inexpensive
physical education
equipment
for children

10   9   8   7   6   5   4   3   2   1

Consulting Editors to the Publisher

Eloise M. Jaeger
University of Minnesota
Minneapolis, Minnesota

Robert M. Clayton
Colorado State University
Fort Collins, Colorado

Illustrations by Scott Earle and Barbara Warrington.

Preface

Teachers in the public schools as well as in various recreational settings often find conditions less than ideal. All too often they must teach large classes with limited equipment. This deprives the children of quantity and quality movement experiences which would allow for the development of stability, locomotor, and manipulative patterns through games, rhythms, and gymnastic activities.

It is the purpose of this book to provide elementary school classroom teachers, physical education specialists, special education teachers, recreation leaders, and parents interested in developing movement experiences with some innovative ideas for constructing and utilizing homemade equipment. Activities which have been found to be interesting to children and adaptable to large classes are suggested. The use of inexpensive equipment will make it possible for each child to have a piece of equipment. As a result, all children will be actively involved in the development of efficient movement patterns.

Special thanks go to Mary Werner, Linda Simmons, Carl Ridenour, and Jane Holloway for their suggestions and contributions to the book.

iii

Contents

CHAPTER 1

Introduction

Purpose of the Book

In many public schools large classes and/or lack of facilities and equipment often cause problems in effectively teaching movement experiences to children in the elementary school, especially in the primary grades. Large classes prevent children from receiving adequate time to explore and manipulate various pieces of equipment because they have to wait their turn. In classes where only one or two pieces of equipment can be found, children get caught in the waiting process also. As a result, they are robbed of quantity and quality movement experiences which would allow for the development of stability, locomotor, and manipulative patterns through games, rhythms, and gymnastics activities. In addition, discipline and control problems often result when children have to wait in lines.

In an attempt to provide a solution to the above problems, teachers and parents should be encouraged to develop homemade physical education equipment. It is the purpose of this book to introduce ideas for the acquisition and construction of inexpensive equipment as well as to provide ideas for activities which are practical for use with preschool and elementary school children.

Equipment for All Children

The nature of homemade equipment stresses the amount of adaptation for use by all children. Changes in the size, weight, shape, etc., of specific pieces of equipment make them more usable by children, young and old, large and small. Commercially produced equipment is not always as adaptable in nature. In addi-

1

tion, homemade equipment may be specially adapted for use by handicapped children. For example, yarn balls may be used with children who have eye-hand coordination problems and are afraid to catch a regular ball for fear of getting hurt. Balance beams and balance boards may be used with children who have balance problems. Many other pieces of equipment included in this book may be adapted for use in special situations. As a result, this book is recommended not only for those who teach the "normal" preschool and elementary school child, but also for those who teach children who have handicapping conditions such as mental retardation, learning disabilities, and physical handicaps.

Use of Innovative Equipment in Physical Education

The use of free and inexpensive materials will allow each child to explore various movement patterns as an individual or in a small group. Innovative equipment is especially adaptable to movement education situations during the primary grades. Children should be encouraged to explore the various movement qualities of space, force, time, and flow as they experience gymnastics, locomotion, and manipulative activities.

Innovative equipment may also be adapted for use in lead-up games to team sports and other movement experiences. It is not, however, the intent of this book to "play down" the importance of regular equipment for physical education. A combination of innovative and manufactured equipment is important to a quality physical education program from kindergarten through grade twelve.

Sources and Construction of Equipment

Many of the items suggested for innovative physical education equipment may be found in the home. Teachers should encourage the children to bring various items from home. Collection boxes should be provided to keep the items sorted according to use. Other throw-away items such as appliance boxes, tires, inner tubes, and lumber scraps are often gladly donated by local department stores, service stations, and lumber companies. Supplies which must be purchased for the construction of low-cost equipment can often be acquired at a school discount from local businesses.

Construction of the various pieces of equipment can be implemented in several ways. Some of the simple pieces of equipment can be made by the children themselves or in conjunction with the science, art, music, and physical education teachers. Other items such as yarn balls, hoops, or jump ropes may be made by concerned parents or volunteer groups from the PTA. Students in home economics classes in sewing may make equipment such as letter and number beanbags as projects. Industrial arts classes in shop and woodworking may make other items such as balance boards, balance beams, or scooter boards. All that is needed is time, effort, concern, and commitment on the part of the children, parents, teachers, and the community!

Contents of the Book

The remaining chapters of the book are concerned with the acquisition, construction, purpose, and suggested activities for the various pieces of innovative physical education equipment. After naming each piece and suggesting ideas for its acquisition and construction, several objectives are listed. Finally, an emphasis has been placed on suggested activities for each piece of equipment.

Chapter 2, *Save Your Junk*, concentrates on equipment which may be constructed from throw-away items in the home. Chapter 3, *No Cost Equipment*, emphasizes equipment which may be constructed from items which may be acquired from local businesses at no charge. Chapter 4, *Low Cost Equipment*, contains suggestions for equipment which may be constructed at a cost which is lower than manufactured equipment with no sacrifice in durability or quality. Innovations in gymnasium and playground concepts are covered in chapters 5 and 6. An appendix is included which lists sources for equipment which may be purchased and used for innovative activities.

CHAPTER **2**

Save Your Junk

Newspapers

Acquisition

Save and store your daily and Sunday newspapers. The children can also bring newspapers from their homes.

Construction

Tear the newspapers in half through the center fold and stack them for the children's use. No further construction is necessary.

Objectives

To develop gross-motor movement abilities including loco-motor, stability, and manipulative skills.

To develop eye-hand and eye-foot coordination.

To integrate movement experiences with concepts in language arts, mathematics, science, and social studies.

Activities with newspapers

1. Let's pretend this paper is your house. Find a place to build your house. Try not to build too close to your neighbor so that you can have a nice front yard and a large back yard in which to play and plant a garden.

    Today is rainy so you'll have to play inside. Go in and sit down in your house. Look under your right knee and find a word. Make sure you know how to spell the word. Can you clap your hands once for each letter? Let me hear all of you clap the number of letters you have in your word. Ready? Go (repeat looking over left shoulder, between legs, etc.). Now look underneath your seat and see if you can find a word that only has one letter. Can you make your body assume the shape of that letter? Find any word in your house which suggests movement or is a word you can imitate. Since it has stopped raining, go next door and visit your neighbor. Take turns playing charades by having one of you perform the movement and the other one try to guess what it is.

2. Go back to your house and take off your shoes and socks. Walk (run, jump, hop, leap, skip, gallop, slide) around your house and let your toes feel the texture of the floor or grass. How does it feel? Warm or cold? Wet or dry? Smooth or rough?

3. Find at least five different ways to hop or jump over the narrow part of your house. Sometimes land only on one body part. Sometimes land on two body parts. Find two different body parts on which to land. Can you land on three different body parts? What about four body parts? Can you lead with different body parts as you jump? Can you jump backwards? Sideways? Can you turn while you are in the air? Find a new way to get from the one side to the other side still passing over the narrow part of your house and not touching it. Make up a sequence of five different ways to pass over the narrow part of your house without touching it. Repeat that sequence over the long part.

4. Now go and visit three of your neighbors. Touch their houses and hop back home. Be sure to touch each house with a different body part. Run and touch ten other houses with your left hand and then return home. Move to ten new houses by jumping over the first, touching the second with a body part of your choice, jumping over the third, etc., and then return home. How many houses did you jump over? How many houses did you touch? That's right—5 + 5 = 10. Move to ten houses again. This time touch two and jump one until you've visited ten neighbors and then go back home. How many did you touch? How many did you jump over? That's right—7 + 3 = 10.

5. Sit down so that your house is in front of you. Your taxes are too high on such a big house so let's make it smaller. Put the short sides together and make your house half as big. Fold it again and again until you have folded it into a short strip like a

ruler. Hold on to each end with your thumb and index finger. While sitting on the floor, move one foot through and back. Then move the other foot through and back. Move both feet through and hold your body in a "V" position and count to three. Repeat the "V" position and count to five. Everybody see how high you can count while holding the "V" position.

6. Still holding on to your house stretch it tall over your head. Can you move around the room in this tall, stretched position? I want to see very tall children.

7. Still holding on to your house bend over and walk keeping your arms straight. Try to kick your house with your toes while you take each step. See if you can jump through your arms and over your house without damaging it.

8. Fold your house again so that it's even more narrow. Twirl your house like a baton as you pass it from one finger to another. Now try to balance your house on one of your fingers in a vertical position. Can you sit down, stand up, and move about the room while balancing your house? Can you move from a sitting position to a lying position while balancing your house? Can you balance your house on other body parts?

9. Sit down on the floor and place your house in front of you. Your tax rebate has enabled you to make your house big again. Can you make it big again by opening it with your toes? Remember that your house damages easily, so be careful.

10. After you have rebuilt your house to its original size and shape you decide you'd rather have a round house than a square house. See if you can use your feet and toes to make your house round like a ball. Make your house as small and as tightly packed as you can.

11. Throw your house up and catch it—right to right, left to left, etc. How many different ways can you find to throw and catch your house? Find five different things to do with your house besides throwing and catching. Perform the same activities with a partner.

12. Place your house on the floor and kick it about the room using very light kicks. Sometimes use your right foot, sometimes your left. Can you alternate kicking with your right foot, running to it, and then kicking it with the left? Can you kick your house back and forth with a partner as you move from

one side of the room to the other? Can you keep your house
in the air using only your feet to volley it? How many times
can you kick it without letting it hit the floor? See how many
times you can keep it in the air while striking it with your
knee. Try the same thing with your head. How high can you
make it go with your head? Using your head, can you pass
your house back and forth with your neighbor?

13. It's time to make your house square again. Sit down and build
it with your toes. Be sure not to damage it. You didn't do a
very good job with the building this time, so the board of
health has condemned it. As I count to ten, see how many
pieces you can tear your house into using only your feet and
toes. Now count how many pieces you have. How many? I am
going to count to ten again. Still using only your feet and toes,
see if you can double the number of pieces you have. How
many?

14. After you have finished counting, I want you to gather all of
the pieces of your house into a small area because we are going
to play a game. Even though all the houses on the block were
condemned and demolished there are still some valuables left.
When I say "Go," I want you to hop about the room taking
other people's valuables in your toes and bringing them back
to your house. All the while others will be trying to take
valuables from your own home, so you must be very fast in
order to gather more valuables than you lose. When I say
"Stop," I want you to count the number of valuables you
have. Ready, go! Stop! How many have more valuables than
they had before we started stealing? How many more? How
many have less? How many did you lose? A discussion of
attitudes toward stealing is suggested as a follow-up activity.

15. The next game involves playing with your neighbor. One
person will hold a valuable in his toes and hop about the room.
The other person will try to chase after that person and grab
the valuable out of his toes with his hands. Ready? Begin.

16. The next game is a team game with the room divided into two
equal halves with a long jump rope. A wastebasket is placed in
each half of the neighborhood. It's time to do your spring
house cleaning. When I give the starting command, everyone is
to carry in their toes as much garbage and waste paper as they
can to the city dump in their respective neighborhood.

Three-quarters of the way through, the children are told they may use their hands to clean house but may only carry one piece of garbage at a time to the dump. The first team that completes the spring house cleaning with no debris left behind is the winner. Group effort is helpful and is to be encouraged.

Balls

Acquisition

Scraps of yarn, ladies' nylon hose, paper, and socks can be used to make various types of balls for manipulative activities to help children overcome fear of the ball while developing ball-handling skills.

Construction

1. Yarn balls are best made with rug yarn. It takes from one to two skeins of yarn to make one ball, depending on the size of the ball desired. To begin constructing a ball cut two cardboard circles 4 to 6 inches in diameter with a 2-inch hole in the center of each. Put the cardboard circles together. Wrap the yarn around both circles through the hole and around until the 2-inch hole is completely filled. Cut the yarn between the cardboard circles with a razor blade all the way around. Place a strong piece of string between the cardboard circles and tie. Cut and remove both pieces of cardboard.

2. Paper balls are made by crumbling up pieces of newspaper or pages of magazines and then using masking tape to retain the round shape.

3. Nylon balls are made by stuffing ladies' nylon hose into old socks until the desired size ball is achieved. Make sure that the nylons are stuffed in snugly so that the ball becomes resilient. Tuck the loose ends of the sock inside the ball and sew the opening shut.

Objectives

To develop creativity in the use of balls.

To develop eye-hand and eye-foot coordination.

To develop fine-motor coordination.

To develop sport and game-playing skills.

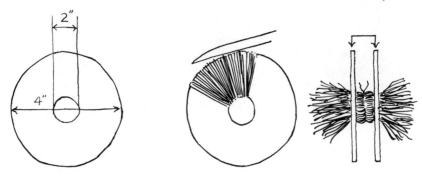

Yarn Ball

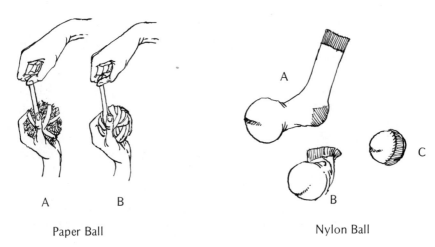

Paper Ball   Nylon Ball

Inexpensive balls can be made from several materials.

Activities with balls

1. Movement exploration.
   a. Find a spot by yourself and see what you can do with the ball while staying in your own space.
   b. Try using different body parts to move the ball and stay in your own space.
   c. Now move the ball around the room anyway you would like, keeping the level of your body and the level of the ball the same, changing these levels frequently.
   d. Use many different body parts this time to move the ball around the room keeping the ball close to you.
   e. How many ways can you make the ball go around you?

    f. What can you do with the ball using one hand? Now try the other hand.

    g. What can your feet do with the ball?

2. Rolling and fielding.

    a. See how many ways you can roll the ball around you changing your base of support often.

    b. How many different directions can you use to roll the ball to yourself?

    c. Roll the ball in a straight line, run after it, and pick it up.

    d. Roll the ball, run after it until you get ahead of the ball, turn around, and pick it up. Try to keep your feet in motion.

    e. Roll the ball, leap over it, turn around, and pick it up by letting it roll up your arms.

    f. Roll the ball against the wall as hard as you want. After it hits, run to meet it, and pick it up.

    g. Roll the ball to a partner, but challenge him by making him move to field it.

    h. In stride position (facing same or opposite directions) roll and field ball between partners.

3. Throwing and catching.

    a. Throw the ball to yourself, showing many different ways you can throw and catch the ball.

    b. How high can you throw the ball and still catch it? How did you make it go higher? Where should you be standing in order to catch the ball easily when it comes down?

    c. How many different ways can you throw the ball without using your hands?

    d. Can you throw the ball up and catch it before it bounces? How many different ways can you move and still catch it?

    e. How many places can you put your hand and catch the ball?

    f. Starting in a standing position, throw the ball up and catch it while you are standing. Do the reverse.

    g. How do you catch the ball most easily, with your arms bent or arms straight? Should you bring the ball in toward your body?

    h. Can you throw the ball up and move somewhere to catch the ball before it bounces?

    i. Can you throw the ball up in the air, turn around, and catch it before it bounces on the floor?

j. Can you throw the ball up in the air and clap two or more times before you catch it?

k. Standing in your own space, see if you can throw the ball behind you and catch it with the same hand.

l. Throw the ball up and catch it without making any noise. As soon as you make contact, give with the ball.

m. Hold the ball out to the side with your arms stretched. Bring the ball over your head and bring the other hand up to meet it to bring the ball down.

n. How many different ways can you get the ball from where you are to the wall?

o. Try to throw the ball with your feet together. Now try it with your feet apart. Try again, this time with a step. Which way did you make your best throw?

p. I see we don't all step out on the same foot. Which foot do you use? Try it with both feet several times. Which way felt best?

q. What direction is your body facing when you start to throw? Does it make any difference in how far or accurately you can throw the ball?

r. Some of us are making our arms follow the ball after it is released and some are not. Try both ways and see which way is best.

s. Try partner activities with throwing and catching balls.

4. Bouncing and dribbling—playground balls are suggested for bouncing.

a. See if you can bounce the ball with both hands with a lot of force.

b. See if you can control the force so that the ball bounces about waist high each time.

c. How many times can you bounce the ball in succession? Try bouncing the ball first with both hands. Now try to bounce the ball with just one hand.

d. Can you bounce the ball best with your right hand or left hand? Can you switch hands without losing control of the ball?

e. How should you use your wrist when you bounce the ball? Is it stiff or does it bounce with the ball? Which way can you bounce the ball the fastest?

f. Can you bounce the ball once and turn around before catching it again? Who can turn around twice?

    g. How low can you bounce the ball? How high can you bounce the ball? Can you bounce it low, then high?

    h. At how many levels can you be while bouncing the ball? Who can be on his stomach while bouncing the ball? Who can sit or be on his back while bouncing the ball? Can you get up while still bouncing it?

    i. See how many different parts of your body can support you while you are bouncing the ball.

    j. In how many directions can you move about the room while you dribble the ball?

    k. Who can run, hop, skip, slide, or gallop while dribbling the ball?

    l. When you move in different directions and dribble, where do you look or focus your eyes?

    m. How many different parts of your body can you use to bounce the ball?

    n. Can you bounce up and down as the ball bounces up and down?

    o. Try to write your initials on the floor with the ball by dribbling in the shape of letters rather than in a straight line.

    p. Get a partner and see how many different ways you can bounce the ball to your partner.

    q. Can you bounce the ball to a partner while you move about the room?

    r. See how you can make your body go over the ball as you give it a bounce with a great deal of force.

    s. See if you can get under the ball in different ways as it is in the air. Try different ways of getting your whole body or body parts under the ball as it is in the air.

5. Volleying.

    a. See if you can keep the ball in the air using different parts of your body to keep it up. You may let it bounce on the floor between contacts. but try not to catch it.

    b. Choose two body parts and see if you can keep the ball in the air by alternating between the two parts.

    c. By yourself, try using parts of your arms or hands to keep the ball in the air.

    d. Now see if you can keep the ball in the air using just your hands and fingers.

    e. Find a space on the wall and see if you can keep the ball rebounding off the wall without catching it.

   f. See if you can volley a yarn ball in the air with forehand and backhand strokes while using an improvised nylon-hose racket. (See page 16.)

   g. Volley a yarn ball back and forth with a partner while using an improvised nylon-hose racket.

6. Foot dribbling and kicking.

   a. See if you can move the ball with your feet without letting it get away from you.

   b. Try using different parts of your feet to move the ball. Use the sole, toes, inside and outside of your feet. Which part of your foot controlled the ball better?

   c. Choose any part of your foot and see if you can change directions as you move the ball around the room.

   d. Kick the ball with a medium amount of force and follow it. Try to stop it with your foot anyway you want without using your hands.

   e. Kick your ball against a wall with any part of your foot and try to make it come directly back to you. When it returns, stop it with your foot or leg. Which part of your foot is most effective for kicking and stopping the ball?

   f. Keeping the ball on the ground, how far can you kick it?

   g. Some children are letting their foot follow the ball after they kick it, while some are stopping their foot when it meets the ball. Try both ways and see which way makes the ball go farther. Which feels better?

   h. What did the foot that did not kick the ball do? What did your arms do? How does this help you kick?

   i. Everyone get a ball but four people. Moving your ball around the room, keeping it close to you, try to keep the students without balls from getting yours.

   j. With a partner (or in groups of four or five) take one or two balls and make up a game which involves sending the ball back and forth with various body parts.

7. Self-testing activities related to ball handling.

   a. Throw at targets on the wall using overhand and underhand throws for accuracy.

   b. Draw a 3-foot square or circle on the floor. While standing in it, throw the ball up high on the wall and catch it on the fly while you remain in the square or circle.

   c. Make two 3-foot squares on the floor about 10 feet apart in the same direction from the wall. Throw the ball against the wall from the first square so that you can catch the rebound while in the second square.

d. Dribble and pass the ball through hula-hoops.

e. Roll the ball, attempting to knock down Indian clubs.

f. Hit the ball against the wall using one or two hands, overhand or underhand. Try side arm with one hand.

g. Throw or kick the ball for distance.

h. How many times can you hit the ball against the wall with a paddle without missing the ball?

i. Dribble around pins in a zigzag manner. Do this with the feet also.

j. Dribble under bars or ropes placed at various levels.

k. Walk on a balance beam and bounce and catch the ball with each step.

8. Other ball-handling activities.

   a. Danish ball rhythms.

   b. Various games, relays, and sports.

Socks Decorated as Puppets

Acquisition

Socks can be found in most households. A variety of colors can be used for the children's amusement. Various sizes should also be used.

Puppets can be made from old socks.

Construction

Felt marking pens can be used to decorate the puppets in a variety of ways. Other types of coloring substances can also be tried. Animal faces, clowns, cartoon characters, and other individuals can be used for decoration. Pieces of yarn can be used for hair, and other creative ideas can be used for decorating the puppets.

Objectives

To give children the opportunity to express themselves through mimicry.

To help children in the development of social skills.

Activities with sock puppets

1. Use the puppets for self-expression activities (each youngster has his own puppet).

2. Use the puppets in story plays (these can be student planned and developed).

3. Use the puppets in games.

Improvised Rackets

Acquisition

One metal coat hanger, one leg from a nylon stocking or hose, and some masking tape or adhesive tape are all that is needed to construct each racket.

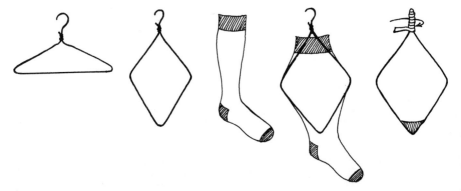

Rackets can be made from coat hangers and nylon hose.

Construction

Bend the hanger into a diamond shape and straighten the hanger hook. Insert the hanger into the hose, making sure to push the end of the hanger snugly into the toe of the stocking. Pull the stocking tightly around the hanger and gather the loose ends by twisting them around the handle. Tape the handle at the base of the diamond. Then bend half of the handle back toward the base of the diamond and tape the whole handle. For greater strength, two hangers and two legs of nylon hose may be used.

Objectives

To develop eye-hand coordination in children.

To develop better striking abilities in children.

To teach teamwork and cooperation through partner and team activities.

Activities with improvised rackets

(Small and/or lightweight balls such as yarn balls or badminton birds work best with this type of racket.)

1. Balance the ball on your racket in forehand and backhand positions and move about the room.

2. Volley the ball into the air 1 or 2 feet continuously while using either the right or left hand in forehand or backhand position. Change hands and change hand positions.

3. Hit the ball into the air as high as you can and still control it.

4. Volley the ball against the wall as many times as you can.

5. Try hitting the ball in different ways—over your head, behind your back, under your legs, etc.

6. Volley the ball back and forth with a partner.

7. As the ball comes to you from your partner, see if you can stop its momentum and make it come to rest on your racket.

8. Given a racket, a ball, and some other pieces of equipment such as a rope or hoop, create a new game with your equipment.

9. Play the game of badminton or modifications of it with your racket.

Plastic Bottles

Acquisition

Empty plastic bottles of all shapes and sizes can be utilized in physical education classes for various uses. Pint, quart, half-gallon, and gallon milk containers, bleach bottles, soap dispensers, and the like may be brought from the home or obtained from the school lunch program.

Construction

Because the plastic bottles can be used in so many ways and construction is so simple, only a brief description of the process will be mentioned along with the illustrations.

1. Boundary markers, goal markers, or obstacle markers can be made by pouring about 2 cups of sand into the bottle (so that the wind won't blow it over) and then painting with various numbers or symbols for the different activities. Keep the caps on the jugs.

2. Plastic bottles can be used as bowling pins. The jugs should be painted and may be stood on the bottom or cap, making it easier for small children to knock them over. Any size jug can be used.

3. Homemade weights can be made by filling the plastic jugs with cement and joining them with aluminum or galvanized lengths of pipe. Drill a ¼-inch hole near the end of the pipe and insert a large nail through the hole. This will prevent the cement from pulling off the pipe. Pour the cement into one of the cans and place the pipe into the mixed cement making sure the pipe is placed in the middle and perpendicular to the bottom of the can. Let this one dry before repeating the process to the other end of the pipe.

4. Plastic bottles may also be used as support aids for beginning swimmers. They may be used individually or joined together with short pieces of rope.

5. A tinikling (Philippine folk dance) set can be made from four plastic jugs (1-gallon size) and two pieces of rope of any desired length. Drill a hole in the center of the bottom of each jug slightly larger than the diameter of the rope. Next insert the rope into the hole and feed it through until it comes out the mouth of the jug. Then tie a large knot in the end and slip

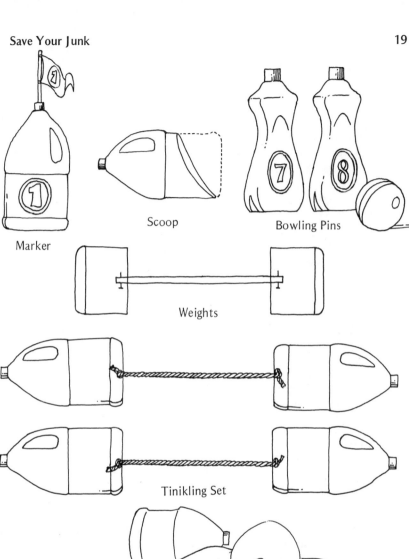

Marker

Scoop

Bowling Pins

Weights

Tinikling Set

Support Aid

Plastic bottles can be used for many kinds of equipment.

it back into the jug. Repeat the procedure with the other end of the rope on another jug. Repeat the procedure with the second rope and remaining jugs.

6. Scoops can be made by cutting the end and/or any part of the side out of the plastic bottles. For protection, place tape around the edges which have been cut. Paint the scoops as desired. All scoops should have the grip-type handles.

Objectives
To develop eye-hand and eye-foot coordination.

To develop manipulative abilities in children.

To develop rhythmical qualities in children.

Activities with plastic bottles

Because the plastic bottles are used primarily for lifting or supporting activities in the first four items in construction above, suggested activities will be limited to uses of the tinikling sets and scoops.

1. Tinikling is a folk dance originating from the Philippine Islands. An album containing tinikling music is RCA Victor—LPM1619. Any record with 3/4 time may be substituted. Originally done with two people striking bamboo poles together at ankle level in an "in, out, out" rhythm pattern, the dance may be executed quite well with the innovative equipment. While the ropes are together, the participants jump with their feet on the outside of the ropes. While the ropes are apart for two counts, the participants jump with their feet on the inside of the ropes. To create a definite rhythmical beat, the plastic bottles should be struck on the floor about shoulder width apart on the two "out" beats. Some possible patterns follow:
   a. Straddle the ropes with both feet on "in." Jump two times with the feet on the inside on the two "out" beats.
   b. Do the same as above, but turn a half turn as you jump while on the inside of the ropes.
   c. Start on the left side of the ropes. On the "in" beat remain on the outside and place your weight on your left foot. On the two "out" beats, jump on the inside with your right foot two times. Continue the pattern—left, right, right, etc.
   d. Do the same as above, only on the right side of the ropes. The pattern will be right, left, left, etc.

    e. Start on the left side of the ropes and transfer to the right side. On the "in" beat place your weight on your left foot. On the first "out" beat jump to the inside with your right foot. On the second "out" beat jump on the inside with your left foot. As the ropes come together again jump to the outside and land on your right foot. Continue the crossing pattern, crossing from one side of the ropes to the other on each new measure.

    f. Think up new patterns and try them on your own!

2. Plastic bottles with the bottoms cut out can be used for many throwing and catching activities. Various sized balls may be used.

    a. Throw the ball up to yourself and catch it with your scoop.

    b. Throw the ball against a wall and catch it on the rebound with your scoop.

    c. First use one hand to catch the ball with the scoop and then try the other hand.

    d. With a partner, throw the ball with the scoop in different overhand and underhand motions and catch the ball with the scoop.

    e. Roll the ball to a partner with the scoop and try to catch the ball with the scoop.

    f. Various modifications of volleyball, basketball, and softball can be developed which utilize the scoop.

Tin Cans

Acquisition

Used tin cans of all sizes from home or the school lunch program can be utilized for many movement experiences in physical education.

Construction

1. When used for relays, stacking, or target purposes, no construction is involved except for taping the rough edges for safety purposes and painting the outside for decorative purposes.

2. When used for golf-putting practice and similar movement experiences, the above preparation of the cans is sufficient. Use small cans for difficult holes and large cans for easier holes.

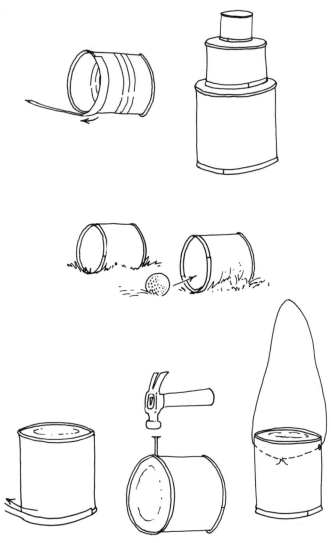

Tin cans have many uses.

3. When preparing cans for "Romper Stomper" activities, the
   #10-size industrial food cans or large coffee cans work best.
   Punch a hole on each side of the can on the end where the lid
   is still intact. Insert one end of a jump rope in each hole and
   tie a knot in each end so that the rope will not pull back
   through the holes. The loop of the rope should be about hip

high. To prevent wear on the rope, wrap tape around the rope where it passes through the holes. Place the plastic lid from the coffee can in the open end of the can or tape the edge so that the floor will not be scratched. Provide two cans for each child.

Objectives

To provide training in eye-hand and eye-foot coordination.

To provide training in gross-motor coordination and agility.

To provide training in fine-motor coordination.

Activities with tin cans

1. Relay, stacking, and target activities.
   a. Use three or more cans placed in a line and have the children run, hop, skip, or use any form of locomotion to zigzag between the cans in the performance of a relay.
   b. Fetch and carry various cans to different points or lines on the gymnasium floor.
   c. Carry or balance different size cans on different body parts during the performance of a relay.
   d. Use a controlled kick, and kick the cans in zigzag fashion around a relay obstacle course.
   e. Stack the cans two, three, four, and five high using the same size cans or graduated cans. Perform as individual activities or in group relays.
      Have the children try to toss small objects into the cans placed at various distances.

2. Golf putting and other movement experiences.
   a. Use golf putters, broom handles, wands, or other striking implements to hit golf balls, wiffle balls, tennis balls, or any other type of balls into cans in a prearranged golf course (eighteen holes) designed on the gymnasium floor.
   b. Use the fingers, hands, elbows, knees, or any other body part to provide the force for guiding the different balls into the holes in a movement exploration situation.

3. "Romper Stomper" activities.
   a. With one can under each foot, while grasping the cords in each hand and holding the cans tightly to the feet, the child should try to walk forward, backward, and sideways using the cans as stilts.

b. Try to perform various hopping or jumping activities while using the cans as stilts.

c. Have the children move through an obstacle course or perform various relay activities while using the tin can stilts.

Garden Hose

Acquisition

Collect pieces of old garden hose from home or purchase desired length of hose from local hardware stores. One plastic coupler for each deck tennis ring is also needed.

Construction

1. Handles for jump ropes can be made by using 4- to 6-inch pieces of garden hose. Tie a knot about 8 inches from each end of the rope. Slide the garden hose onto the end of the rope. Tie a second knot at the end of the rope so that the handle fits securely. Cut away any loose ends.

2. Rings for tossing or playing deck tennis may be constructed by cutting a piece of garden hose into 18- to 24-inch lengths and joining the ends with plastic couplers or taping the ends securely with adhesive tape.

3. Partner and multiple tug-of-war ropes may be constructed by using the garden hose as handles on heavy sash cord to prevent rope burns. For individual ropes use 10 feet of sash cord. Slip about 12 to 18 inches of garden hose over each end of the rope and tie the rope in loop fashion as shown in the picture. Multiple tug-of-war ropes may be constructed by securely attaching a garden-hose handle to one end of an 8-foot length of rope and the opposite end of the rope to a strong ½-inch metal ring or old gymnastics spotting belt as illustrated in the picture.

Objectives

To develop eye-hand and eye-foot coordination in the various throwing, catching, and jumping activities.

To develop static and dynamic strength in the arms, trunk, and legs.

To develop balance, agility, and reaction-time abilities.

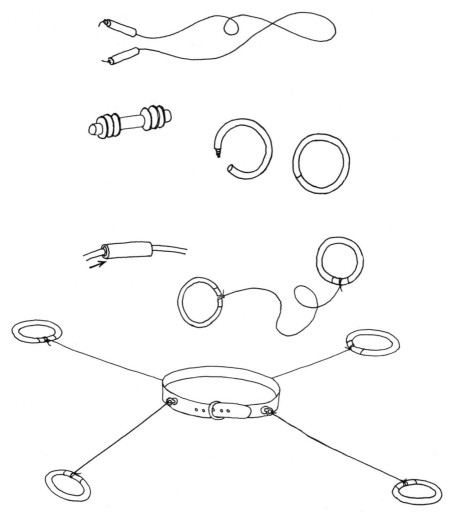

Pieces of garden hose can be used for many pieces of equipment.

To develop partner and team cooperation in the activities involving deck tennis and multiple tug-of-war struggles.

Activities involving garden hose

1. Jump ropes—refer to the section on jump ropes (page 86).

2. Ring toss and deck tennis.
   a. Throw the ring up in the air and catch it yourself in several different ways. Use both hands.

    b. Throw the ring toward a peg or small plastic bottle and aim it so that it lands over the object.

    c. Throw the ring back and forth with a partner. Throw and catch the ring in different ways.

    d. Adapt the team game of deck tennis to the abilities of the children. Use a badminton net, volleyball net, or rope as a net to throw over.

3. Ring wrestling using the garden-hose ring. This activity is suitable for children in grades four to six. As the activity is combative in nature, the children should be matched by height and weight. Time of the matches can vary from 10 to 30 seconds (maximum of 30 seconds).

Important Teaching Point: Children should remain on their knees throughout the match, and they must stop the match on signal.

    a. Begin kneeling side by side, try to get the ring on your partner's foot.

    b. Repeat, but put the ring over your partner's other foot.

    c. Repeat the same problem, but change beginning position: back to back kneeling, back-lying, sitting back to back, etc.

    d. Each player hold the ring with one hand; attempt to get it over the other player's foot.

    e. Repeat item *d* but begin by holding ring with both hands.

    f. Repeat items *a-e* but use the "referee's position" (from high school wrestling). The ring can be held by either player.

    g. Try other variations of combative movements with the ring.

This activity can be quite vigorous and should be used with rest periods. The teacher should control the activity at all times.

These matches should be conducted on tumbling mats.

4. Partner and multiple tug-of-war ropes.

    a. Using individual ropes try to pull your partner across the line or out of a circle using right hand, left hand, both hands, face to face, back to back, and other variations.

    b. Using three or four bases of support try to pull your partner off balance by placing either hand or foot through the loop of the rope and tugging as strong as you can.

    c. Repeat the above activities but have each child try to pick up an object that is behind him.

  d. Perform sit-ups using partner opposition by holding on to the ends of the ropes.
  e. Use multiple ropes and tug two against two, three against three, etc.
  f. Using multiple ropes, repeat some of the partner activities listed above.
  g. Perform isometric exercise using partner or multiple ropes. Try various body positions and angles with the limbs of the body. Hold each position for six to eight counts before assuming another isometric position.

Milk Cartons and Paper Tubing

Acquisition

Milk cartons and paper tubing from rolls of wax paper, paper towels, or various sizes of rolls of paper can be found in the home and brought to school to be used in physical education for a variety of purposes.

Construction

When the milk cartons and paper tubing are used for bowling pins, goals, relays, and other movement experiences, no construction is involved except for painting and decorating the outside with various colors, numbers, geometric designs, letters, and pictures. When used for throwing, catching, and kicking experiences, no construction is involved either. However, selected catching and rolling experiences designed to develop eye-hand

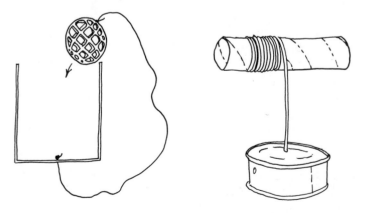

Examples of equipment made from milk cartons and paper tubing.

coordination and arm strength involve the attachment of a string and ball to the cartons and tubing. In the first instance, punch a hole in the bottom of the milk carton, pass a string through the hole, and tie a knot on the inside. Attach a ball on the free end of the string as shown in the picture. Then swing the ball up and try to catch it in the carton. In the second instance, attach a string to the middle of the paper tubing as shown in the picture. Attach a ball to the free end of the string and try to roll the ball up to the tubing using forward and backward motions.

Objectives

To develop eye-hand coordination.

To develop arm strength.

Activities with milk cartons and paper tubing

1. Bowling pins. Use from one to ten cartons at a time while children try to roll balls and knock the cartons over.

2. Use the cartons to designate goals in various games or various distance markers for throwing or kicking activities.

3. Relays.
   a. Use in fetch-and-carry relays.
   b. Stack one on top of another in a relay activity.
   c. Use as markers to dodge in an obstacle course relay.

4. Throwing, catching, and carrying.
   a. Balance a carton or tube on various body parts as you move about the room.
   b. Set up the cartons or tubes in a miniature golf course and try to shoot small balls such as ping-pong balls into the openings of the cartons with your fingers and other body parts.
   c. Try to throw the cartons or tubes as if you were passing a football.
   d. Try to kick the cartons or tubes as if you were kicking a football.

5. Try to swing a ball attached to a string into the carton in several different body positions. Use both hands.

6. Roll the ball up the paper tubing in both forward and backward motions.

Plastic Lids

Acquisition

Large-size plastic lids from coffee or fruit cans can be used for several activities in physical education. Small pieces of sash cord or rope and old tennis balls or plastic tops from spray cans are additional scraps which are needed to make "footsies."

Construction

Left untouched, large plastic lids can be adapted to Frisbee activities. With the center cut out, the plastic lids can be adapted to ring toss or deck tennis games. To make "footsies," cut the center out of a plastic lid to make the ring. Cut a piece of rope 18 to 24 inches in length. Use an old tennis ball or plastic top from a spray can to make the weighted end of the "footsie." Tie the rope to the edge of the plastic lid. Poke a hole on the top of the spray can lid, run the rope through, and tie a knot.

Objectives

To develop eye-hand and fine-motor coordination.

To develop eye-foot coordination.

To develop throwing and catching abilities in children.

Activities with plastic lids

1. Frisbee activities.
   a. See if you can sail the Frisbee into the air so that it will return to you.
   b. With a partner, sail the Frisbee back and forth to one another.
   c. See if you can make the Frisbee bounce off the ground and into your partner's hands as you sail the Frisbee.
   d. See if you can sail the Frisbee to your partner as you move about the room.
2. Ring toss or deck tennis activities.
   a. Set up small targets such as pop bottles or liquid soap containers and try to throw the rings over the targets from a distance of 3 to 6 feet.
   b. Set up a badminton or volleyball net, divide the children into teams, and play deck tennis by throwing the ring back and forth across the net.

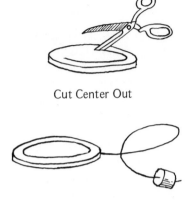

Cut Center Out

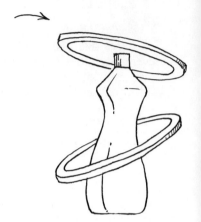

Attach weighted rope to plastic lid.

Ring Toss

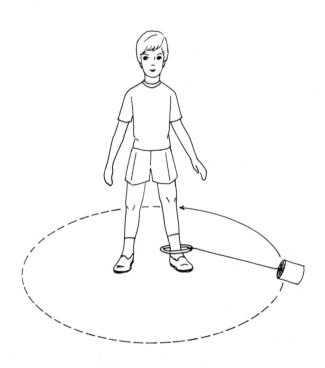

Examples of how plastic lids can be used.

3. Footsie activities.
   a. Skip the footsie with your right or left foot in place.
   b. Skip the footsie with your right or left foot as you travel about the room forward, backward, or sideways.
   c. Skip with one footsie on each foot.
   d. Skip with one footsie on either foot as you twirl a footsie on each arm.
   e. Skip with one footsie on each foot as you twirl a footsie on each arm.
   f. Combine one-foot travel while you twirl a footsie on your arms.
   g. Skip the footsie with your right or left foot as you bounce a ball.
   h. Twirl the footsie with your arms using different patterns: figure eight, horizontal, vertical, in front of your body, and to the side of your body.

Paper Plates

Acquisition

Paper plates may be purchased any any local grocery store or brought from home by teachers or children.

Construction

For certain balancing activities no construction is involved other than perhaps painting designs or faces on the plates. For some tossing activities, the center disk of the plate may be cut out. Other activities utilizing the paper plate involve the construction of a cone for throwing and catching activities. To construct the cone, make a slit from the edge to the center of the paper plate and overlap the edges about 5½ inches. Secure the edges with paper fasteners and attach 6 inches of ¼-inch elastic cord to the fasteners. Stick a paper fastener in the center of the plate and attach 5 inches of the elastic cord to the fastener. The length of the elastic will vary, depending upon the size of the child. Notch the plate between the two paper fasteners to help keep the plate from sliding off the ankle or wrist.

Objectives

To develop eye-hand and eye-foot coordination in children.

To develop laterality, directionality, and spatial awareness in children.

To develop rhythmical abilities and awareness in children.

To encourage children to cooperate when involved in partner activities.

Activities with paper plates

1. Balancing activities.
    a. Balance the plate on your head and try to walk about the room.
    b. Balance the plate on other body parts such as your wrist or finger tips as you walk about the room.
    c. Use different bases of support such as arms, elbows, and knees as you balance the plate with your body.
    d. Use various forms of locomotion such as crab walk, hop, or skip as you balance the plate with your body.
    e. Work with a partner and balance the plate between you as you move about the room.

2. Tossing activities.
    a. Toss the plate into the air and catch it as it comes down.
    b. Toss the plate to a partner as if you were throwing a Frisbee.
    c. With the center disk cut out, try to throw the plate over plastic bottles which are placed at various distances.

3. Paper cone activities.
    a. With the cone attached to one foot, place a yarn ball in the cone and balance it as you walk in different directions.
    b. With the cone attached to one foot, place a ball in the cone and balance it as you use other forms of locomotion to move about the room.
    c. With the cone attached to one foot, try to drop a ball from your hand and catch it in the cone.
    d. With the cone attached to one foot, try to play catch with a partner by tossing the balls from hand to foot, foot to hand, or foot to foot.
    e. With the cone attached to one wrist, either on the backhand or forehand, perform the activities in *a* and, *b* above.
    f. With the cone attached to one wrist, toss a ball into the air and catch it in the cone.
    g. With the cone attached to one wrist, try to play catch with a partner.

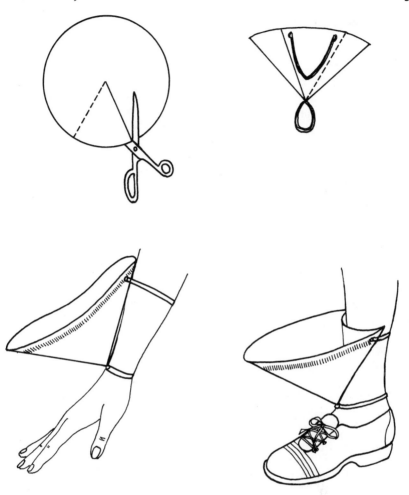

Paper plate cones can be used for catching objects.

h. Attempt to perform relays of all types by utilizing the cone attached to the foot or wrist.[1]
i. Play simple games such as Red Light or Freeze Tag while balancing a ball in the cone attached to the foot or wrist.

[1]Werner, Peter H., and Losh, George, "A Paper Plate Cone for Elementary Physical Education," *Journal of Health, Physical Education, and Recreation* 44:72-74, January, 1973.

Eye-Hand Coordination

Acquisition

Objects such as washers, nuts and bolts, hinges, Mason caps from jars, egg cartons, and the like can be collected and used for movement experiences in physical education. All materials may be found in the home and donated to the school by willing parents.

Construction

No construction is involved except for decorating items with various designs or colors. This may be accomplished in cooperation with the art teacher.

Objectives

To develop eye-hand coordination.

To develop manipulative skills.

To develop fine-motor coordination in the hands.

Activities with objects to develop eye-hand coordination

1. Washers and bottle caps.
   a. Toss them into cans, egg cartons, and the like from various distances.
   b. String them on a coat hanger to make a tambourine.
   c. Play checkers or tic-tac-toe with them.
   d. Play finger shuffleboard or caroms.
   e. Play tiddly-winks with them.

2. Nuts and bolts. Show children how to turn the nut on the bolt using just the fingers and then have races tightening and loosening the bolt. Use various sizes.

3. Hinges, latches, hooks, zippers, belts, buttons, etc. Make a special board with common household and everyday tasks attached to the board. Children can then learn how to perform tasks such as tying shoes, buckling belts, latching doors, and the like in a guided exploration setting.

4. Mason caps. Experiences similar to the washer experiences above may be performed.

5. Egg cartons.
   a. Balance the carton on different body parts as you move about the room using different bases of support.
   b. Line several cartons in a line and then jump, hop, or perform other locomotor movements from one side to the other.
   c. Use the cartons as goals or boundary markers.
   d. Hold the carton in your hands and use it to catch washers or small balls which are thrown to you. Try catching them in specific sections of the carton by giving each space a number from one through twelve.
   e. Use the cartons for fetch-and-carry relays for pushing about the room with various body parts for exploration experiences.

6. Pop cans.
   a. Use the cans for fetch-and-carry relays.
   b. Use the cans as markers in tin can bowling.
   c. Play telephone with two cans attached by a string.
   d. Put stones in cans and use for a rhythm band.
   e. Play "kick the can" or other football games by wrapping the can in old rags.
   f. Toss objects such as buttons or bottle caps in the cans.
   g. Roll the can across the floor with a broom stick in relay races.
   h. Play ice hockey, field hockey, or other games by adapting the game to the use of a can.

7. Coat hangers.
   a. Hang coat hangers on a rope and transfer hangers from one end of the rope to the other in relay fashion while solving mathematics problems.
   b. Punch holes in bottle caps and string on the coat hangers to make tambourines for rhythm bands.
   c. Hang up old clothes in a relay activity.

8. Clothes pins and magnets attached to strings.
   a. Pick up small objects on the floor with the clothes pins or magnets.
   b. Attach clothes pins to a line in a relay activity.

Broom Sticks and Mop Handles

Acquisition

The handles of broken or worn out brooms and mops may be collected from home, school, or industry and used for a variety of purposes in physical education.

Construction

1. For various striking activities, leave the broom intact and use the head as the striking surface.

2. For various wand activities, cut the head off the broom or mop so that it is 3 to 4 feet in length.

3. For lummi stick activities, cut the broom or mop handles into lengths of 8 to 12 inches.

Objectives

To develop various aspects of physical fitness such as balance, flexibility, agility, and strength.

To develop eye-hand and eye-foot coordination.

To develop various rhythmical and time/space qualities in children.

Activities with broom sticks and mop handles

1. Whole brooms.
    a. Ride the broom like a horse.
    b. Play various hockey games by using the broom as a stick and a wiffle ball, shaving can top, or similar object as a puck.
    c. Use the broom as a bat for stick ball.

2. Wands.
    a. Balance the wand on your hand, head, or another body part in a horizontal position as you move about the room.
    b. Balance the wand in a vertical position on various body parts.
    c. Balance the wand on the floor in a vertical position. Release grasp, turn around 360°, and regrasp before the wand falls to the floor.
    d. Stand a wand on one end and hold on to it. Bring one of your feet over the stick, letting go of it and catching it again before it falls to the ground.

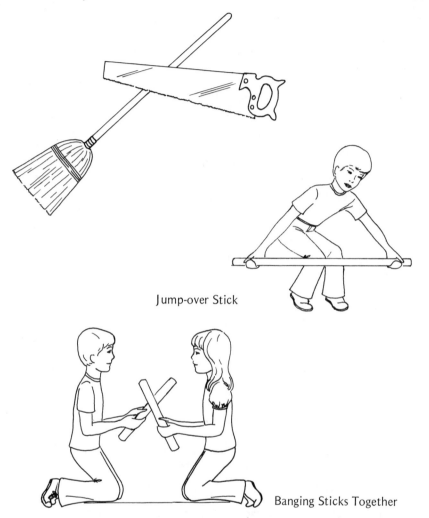

Jump-over Stick

Banging Sticks Together

Broom sticks and mop handles can be adapted for many uses.

   e. With a partner, balance your wand on the floor in a vertical position. Release the grasp of your wand and catch your partner's wand before it falls and jump over it.

   f. Roll the wand on the floor and jump over it.

   g. Place several wands on the floor at varying distances apart and hop or jump over the wands while varying your direction, level, speed, or force of movement.

   h. Hold on to the wand at each end and jump through the arms and over the wand without releasing your grip.

i. Have a partner rotate a wand around himself at a level near the floor. Jump the wand as it passes under your feet.

j. Grasp the wand with your arms apart. Keeping your arms straight, pass the wand over your head and down to the back.

k. Grasp the wand with both hands, palms facing away from your body. Step over the wand with one leg at a time. Bring the wand over the head. Step around one arm with the leg on the same side. Place the leg that went around the arm between you and the wand. Pull on the wand until it is all the way over your back and head. Finally, step over the wand until you are back to the original position in which you started.

l. Hold the wand in a vertical position with the end of the wand on the floor. Twist so that you pass under the arm holding the wand without letting go of the wand, taking it off the floor, or touching your knee to the floor.

m. Throw the wand as far as you can as if you were throwing a javelin.

n. Twirl the wand as if it were a baton.

o. Walk on the wand placed on the floor as if it were a tightrope.

p. Perform a cartwheel or other leaping, hurdling, and jumping stunts over the wand.

q. With a partner sitting or standing on a carpet sample or gym scooter and holding on to a wand, pull him around the floor.

r. Try to perform limbo stunts by passing under a wand held at levels closer and closer to the floor.

s. Have partners play tug-of-war while grasping the wand in several different positions. For example, try holding the wand while you are face to face, back to back, or place the wand between your legs.

t. Try wrestling a wand away from your partner. The wand should be gripped so that the children's hands are alternately placed. On command, each child tries to make the other child let go of the wand by twisting the wand back and forth and applying pressure.

u. With a partner, hold on to the wand as in the same activity as above. On command, each child tries to touch the right end (his right side) of the wand to the ground. Whoever touches his end to the ground is the winner.

    v. With each partner holding on to the wand and crossing the wands in the middle, try to push your opponent off balance or across a line that is drawn behind each person (about 3 feet).

    w. Divide the class into relay teams. Have them run a designated distance, place the wand on the floor with the palm of one hand on top of the wand, and rotate around the wand three times (Dizzy Izzy). Each person takes his turn.

    x. Perform other relays by balancing the wand on various body parts, carrying the wand, or using the wand to strike objects on the floor through an obstacle course.

    y. Attach a weight on the end of a rope to the wand. Try to roll the weight up to the wand by using forward and backward rolling motions.

3. Lummi sticks[2] or batons.

    a. Use the lummi sticks as batons for relay passing in track and field.

    b. Tap the head of one or both sticks to the floor to the beat of the music.

    c. Tap the heel of one or both sticks to the floor to the beat of the music.

    d. While sitting on the floor with your legs spread apart tap the sticks between your legs, both to the right, both to the left, one on each side, or cross arms and tap one on each side.

    e. Hit the sticks together to the rhythm of the music in the air while changing the position of the sticks in relation to your body.

    f. Flip one or both sticks into the air and catch them to the rhythm of the music.

    g. With a partner, tap your sticks to the rhythm of the music using any of the above patterns (b-c). Try to make up a symmetrical sequence of eight, sixteen, or twenty-four counts which you can repeat.

    h. With a partner, tap your sticks together to the rhythm of

---

[2] Lummi stick rhythms may be done to any music having a basic 4/4 rhythm. Each movement corresponds to one count. Depending on the speed desired, the children may keep time to the first beat of each measure, the first and third beat of each measure, or each beat of the measure.

the music. Tap right to right, left to left, right to left, left to right, or cross the sticks and tap both at the same time.

i. With a partner, flip your sticks to each other to the rhythm of the music. Flip right to left, left to right, right to right, left to left, or both sticks at the same time.

Paper Strip Streamers

Acquisition

Crepe paper or newspaper in any variety of colors may be used for this type of activity.

Construction

Cut the strips so that they are from 1 to 2 inches in width and from 4 to 10 feet in length.

Objectives

To develop rhythmical qualities in children.

To explore various qualities of space, force, time, and flow through discovery experiences.

To develop the ability of children to work together as partners or to make up a short dance with the use of streamers.

Activities with streamers

1. Move the streamer to the rhythm of the music without touching it to the floor.

2. Move anywhere making your streamer fly sometimes high and sometimes low.

3. Find out what happens to your streamer when you make sudden changes of direction.

4. Use leaping and spinning movements with your streamer.

5. Experiment with spinning movements while your body weight is supported by body parts other than your feet.

6. Hold the streamer with different body parts while you move through space.

7. Make different shapes with your streamer in the air.

8. Make your streamer stay close to you and then far away from you.

Streamers facilitate rhythmical experiences.

9. With a partner, develop a sequence so that you change streamers.

10. Use changes in level and force as you develop a sequence with your partner.

11. Make your streamers use similar, different, and opposite air patterns as you develop your sequence.

12. Make your streamer move about your partner as you move.

13. Try to move through your partner's streamer as it moves.

14. Make up a short dance with the streamers showing very strong and very light movement.

Musical Instruments

Acquisition

Strainers, cans, coat hangers, sand paper, bottle caps, pots and pans, spoons, Mason caps, drum sticks, cardboard boxes, beans, peas, bells, TV dinner trays, plastic bottles, and other throw-away items can be brought from home to make musical instruments for use in physical education.

Bell Bracelet

Maracas Made from
Two Strainers

Maraca Made from
Plastic Bottle

Tambourine of
Bottle Caps and
Washers

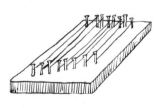

Stringed Instrument

Glass Jars
with Water

Many types of rhythmical instruments can be constructed.

Xylophone

Maracas Made from Two
Paper or Pie Plates

Dried Corn or Peas Inside

Triangle and Nail

Rhythm Sticks

Flattened Bottle Caps

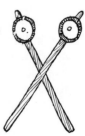

*Construction_*

Bells can be attached together on a string and placed around the head, arm, or leg for various rhythmical experiences. Two strainers can be attached together with wire. Beans are placed on the inside to make a maraca. Faces or designs can be painted on the outside for effect. Two TV dinner trays, paper plates, or pie tins attached together in the same way with beans on the inside elicit the same sound. Other hollow cardboard boxes or plastic bottles can be partially filled and shaken to elicit the same sound. Hollow cardboard boxes or plastic bottles may also be used as drums. Spoons, sticks, cans, pots and pans, and pieces of metal or wood can be struck together to achieve various percussive sounds. Sand paper or other abrasive materials can be rubbed together for other percussive sounds. Washers, bottle caps, or Mason caps can be strung on a coat hanger to make a tambourine. Monofilament fishing line of assorted pound tests or rubber bands can be stretched between nails of varying distances to achieve musical notes of different pitches. Various sizes of glass jars may be filled with water to different levels and struck with objects to achieve musical notes of graduated pitch also. A xylophone may be constructed out of pieces of wood or ceramics by attaching and suspending different length pieces in order of size or density on a string.

Objectives

To develop an awareness of rhythms and time/space relationships.

To provide for integrative experiences with the performing arts.

To develop eye-hand coordination and eye-foot coordination.

Activities with musical instruments

When initiated in cooperation with the music and art teachers, a whole unit of integrated experiences can evolve. Instruments can be made in art class. The elements of music such as beat, measure, accent, tempo, and the like can be taught by the music teacher and in physical education. The children can learn to play their instruments and move creatively to the sound of their own modern rhythm band tunes.

CHAPTER 3

No Cost Equipment

Appliance Boxes

Acquisition

Appliance boxes can be obtained at nearly any appliance or department store. Other large boxes of this type may also be used.

Construction

The boxes can be painted a variety of colors or they can be covered with "contact" paper. Many of the geometric shapes can be cut in the sides of the boxes. Squares, rectangles, circles, triangles, hexagons, and octagons are examples of the shapes that can be cut in the boxes. Numbers and letters can also be cut. All of the openings should be large enough so that small children can crawl in and out.

Objectives

To help children develop spatial awareness.

To help children develop an understanding of geometric shapes.

To help children develop eye-hand coordination.

Activities with appliance boxes

1. Each child can crawl in and out of the boxes, using any of the openings.

2. Each child can use the openings as targets for beanbag or ball toss.

3. The boxes can be used as part of a maze or obstacle course.

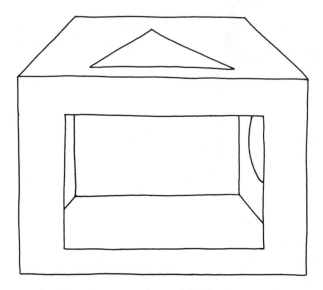

Appliance boxes can be used for form perception.

4. Relay races can be run through or around the boxes.

5. Two or more children can make up games with the appliance boxes (use balls, hoops, beanbags, etc.).

Automobile Tires

Acquisition

Old tires may be obtained at any service station or junkyard.

Construction

None necessary, unless the tires need to be scrubbed for indoor use.

Objectives

To help children develop spatial awareness.

To help children develop balance.

To help children develop eye-hand coordination.

To help children develop manipulation skills.

Automobile tires encourage gross-motor movement.

Activities with tires

1. Crawl through one tire.

2. Crawl through two or more tires while they are held upright.

3. Roll the tire.

4. Roll the tire; run and jump over the rolling tire; turn and stop the rolling tire.

5. Roll the tire; run in front of the tire and stop it.

6. Roll and catch the tire with a partner.

7. Spin the tire like a coin; as it settles to the floor run around it as many times as possible before it stops.

8. Bounce on the tire; use it as a mini-trampoline.

9. Bounce from tire to tire in a pattern.

10. Hop in and out of individual tires; set the tires in a pattern and hop in and out of tires. (Line, circle, zigzag, etc.)

11. Extend the body through the tire and roll over and over.

12. Sit on the tire (upright) and balance.

13. Use the tire as a weight; pick it up and raise it as high as possible.

14. Use the tire as a target for beanbag toss, yarn ball toss, or play-ground-ball toss (stationary).

15. Use the tire as a target (moving) by hanging it from a basket support with a rope; as the tire swings, throw beanbags or balls through the tire. Make up a game.

16. Many of the listed activities can be used in *obstacle courses.*

17. Various playground activities can be developed.

18. Make tire tunnels for the children to crawl through (varied patterns).

These activities should get you started. Be creative and see if you can *double* the list! Try to collect tires of various sizes.

Bamboo Poles

Acquisition

Bamboo poles (approximately 8 to 10 feet long, 1 or 2 inches in diameter) can be obtained from nearly any rug or furniture company. The poles are often used as center rods for carpet rolls. A pair of poles is needed for every three students. Three or more students can participate in the tinikling dance. Plastic tubing can be substituted for the bamboo poles.

Construction

None needed.

Objectives

To help children develop leg muscles.

To help children develop rhythm and timing.

To help children develop agility and overall coordination.

To help children develop social skills.

Activities with bamboo poles

1. Tinikling —folk dance from the Philippines.
    a. Two students are needed to beat the rhythm with the poles; one is seated at each end of the poles.
    b. One student is the performer and stands beside the poles, halfway from the ends.
    c. Using a 3/4 rhythm, the "pole" students tap the poles on the boards (2 by 4 feet) with an in-out-out, in-out-out, in-out-out pattern.
    d. The same 3/4 pattern is repeated continuously.

    e. The "pole" students should continue the tapping until they get the feel of the beat and at that point add any good 3/4 music for the dance. (An original version of the tinikling music is available from several record companies.) companies.)

    f. The performer may begin the dance as soon as he can accomplish the following steps.

      (1) Straddle the poles on the first beat.

      (2) Jump between the poles for two counts while the poles are apart.

      (3) Return both feet to straddle position as the poles return together for the first beat of the next measure. (Have weight ready to transfer just *ahead* of each move.)

      (4) Standing beside the poles, the performer can hop on one foot (for two counts) between the poles and then return to the outside of the poles with one hop on the other foot. On the *one* hop, the performer should always have his weight ready to transfer *back* to the two hops between the poles.

      (5) The established pattern is in-in-out, in-in-out, in-in-out, etc. Two hops occur between the poles; one hop occurs outside of the poles.

      (6) From the *right* side of the poles the pattern is R-R-L, R-R-L, R-R-L, etc.

      (7) From the *left* side of the poles the pattern is L-L-R, L-L-R, L-L-R, etc.

    g. Once the basic pattern is learned, the performer can travel from side to side and establish a variety of routines.

    h. More than one performer can dance at one time.

2. Other uses.

    a. Poles may be used as crossbars for limbo routines.

    b. Poles may be used in obstacle courses.

    c. Poles may be used for line markings for outside games.

Barrels

Acquisition

Activities with large cardboard barrels can be great fun. The barrels are of very heavy, thick cardboard material and can usually

Barrels can be used for balance.

be obtained from cardboard companies or paper mills. Paper mills would normally have these barrels, as they are the center cores for the large rolls of paper.

Construction

The barrels may be painted a variety of colors. Letters, numbers, and geometric shapes can also be added.

Objectives

To help children develop balance.

To help children develop agility.

To help children develop directionality (right—left).

Activities with barrels

1. Different ways to push the barrel.
   a. Push the barrel with just the right or just the left hand.
   b. Push the barrel with both hands.
   c. Push the barrel with both feet.
   d. Push the barrel with only one foot.
   e. Push the barrel with the other foot.

2. Different ways to balance on the barrels.
   a. Balance on the barrel with both feet.
   b. Walk on the barrel; move forward.
   c. Walk on the barrel; move backward.
   d. Jump on and off the barrel while it is stationary.
   e. While the barrel is moving forward, bring it to a stop, jump, and turn around.
   f. Jump rope while on the barrel.
   g. Bounce a ball while on the barrel.
   h. Work out partner routines on the barrel.
   i. Lie on stomach or back and balance on top of the barrel.

3. Ways to use the barrels as they stand on end.
   a. Use the barrels for target toss with balls, beanbags, and other objects.
   b. Line up the barrels in a row and then as barriers for zigzag running, skipping, hopping, dribbling a ball, and other challenges.
   c. Use the barrels for obstacle courses.
   d. With ends open, the children can crawl through the barrels.

Carpet samples can be used for locomotor experiences.

Carpet Samples

Acquisition

Carpet samples should be at least 12 inches square for use in these activities. Sixteen-inch squares are very effective. Large carpet stores, as well as smaller neighborhood stores, are good sources for acquiring the pieces. Trips to several stores might be necessary to obtain your supply.

Construction

If the 12- by 12-inch or 16- by 16-inch pieces are not available, it is possible to obtain larger sizes and cut them in a variety of squares or rectangles. The carpets can be stacked for storage and the edges sprayed with hair spray to prevent fraying.

Objectives

To help children develop arm and shoulder strength.

To help children develop balance.

To help children develop rhythm.

To help children develop coordination.

To help children develop social skills with partners or in small groups.

Activities with carpet samples

1. Individual.
   a. Skate or ski by putting one rug under each foot. Keep feet well apart for balance. Use arms for skiing or skating motion.
   b. Place knees in the middle of the carpet and pull forward with hands and arms.
   c. Sit in the middle of the carpet and push with the feet and legs. Hands may also be used.
   d. Sit in the middle of the carpet and pull with feet and legs.
   e. Use a body twist to move the carpet. By keeping the feet in the middle of the carpet the student can twist in many different ways. Using music makes this activity even more enjoyable.
   f. Assume a push-up position, with hands on the floor and feet on the carpet. Move forward by "walking" the hands as the feet stay on the carpet. This can be called the seal crawl.
   g. Use two carpets and move by placing the hands on one carpet and knees on the other.
   h. Lie down with back flat on the carpet. Use feet and legs to push the carpet.
   i. With both feet on the carpet use a jumping motion to move forward or backward. Grip the carpet with the feet.
   j. Allow the children to have a "creative" time where they can explore many, many additional movements.

2. Partners.
   a. With one student seated (crossed legs), have the partner carefully pull his mate by his hands. Insist that the students hold both hands and stay on the carpet.
   b. Tag and games of chase may be used with carpets.
   c. One child sits with his feet on one carpet and his seat on the other. His partner uses a jump rope (or other rope) to pull his mate. Best leverage takes place with the rope around the waist of the person pulling.
   d. Try all types of races and relays with the carpets.
   e. Small groups of children may work together in forming patterns, shapes, designs, and movements with the carpets.

3. Other uses or suggestions.
   a. Use the carpets as targets for beanbag toss.
   b. Cut the carpets into geometric shapes and use with correlation activities.
   c. Use rubber-backed carpet for goals, bases, and markers.
   d. Stress safety at all times.
   e. Best movement occurs with the carpet-side *down*.
   f. Try to keep the children on the carpet at all times.

Large Inner Tubes (Car, Tractor, or Truck)

Acquisition

Large inner tubes can be obtained from junkyards, tire dealers, farm implement stores, or from farms. Any large size could be used, and the tube should hold air. Patches might be necessary. Caution should be taken by covering the valve stem so that it does not scratch or puncture a child.

Construction

None needed.

Objectives

To help children be more creative.

To help children develop spatial awareness.

To help children develop leg and arm muscles.

To help children develop agility and coordination.

To help children develop rhythm and timing.

Activities with large inner tubes

1. Refer to section on "Tires" in this chapter (page 46).
2. Other uses.
   a. Use the tube for two-, four-, or six-person tug-of-war.
   b. Tie a rope to the tube and pull a partner as he sits on (or in) the tube.
   c. Walk on the tube while it is lying on the floor.
   d. Make up games with the tube (s).

Bicycle Inner Tubes

Acquisition

Bicycle repair shop; collection boxes at school.

Bicycle inner tubes can be used for group movement experience.

Construction

Use adhesive tape to tape the valve stem to the tube.

Objectives

To help children develop flexibility.

To help children develop muscles through isometric and isotonic exercises.

To help children develop body awareness (body parts).

To help children develop social interaction.

To help children have fun and enjoyment.

Activities with bicycle inner tubes

1. Individual activities (most of these should be held for six counts).
   a. Stand with both feet on the inner tube, and pull up with both arms (palms down).

b. Same as item *a* but reverse grip (palms up).
c. Stand with both feet on the tube; loop the tube behind the neck; from a crouch position force the tube up with the neck.
d. Same as item *c* but push arms out to the side.
e. Double the tube; loop the tube around one foot; balance on one foot; pull to the *side* with the other foot.
f. Repeat item *e* using the other foot.
g. Double the tube; stand on the tube with one foot; pull the tube *up* with the other foot.
h. Repeat item *g* using the other foot.
i. Double the tube; hook behind one heel; keep other leg straight; point toe and lift leg straight forward; hold six counts.
j. Repeat item *i* using the other foot.
k. Double the tube; hold high over the head with straight arms; pull for six counts.
l. Double the tube; hold in front of the body with arms straight; pull for six counts.
m. Using two doubled tubes, place one under each foot; pull up with hands and walk with stiff legs.

2. Partners.
a. Sit with feet flat against partners; hook tube over feet; keep legs straight and use rowing technique; lie down, sit up, lie down, sit up, etc.

Bicycle inner tubes can be
used for resistance activities.

   b. With tube around waist of both partners, have each partner
      take four steps out, four steps in.
   c. Make up a creative movement with your partner.
   d. What other partner stunts can be done?
 3. Groups of four.
   a. With tube held in hands, two partners stay in place while
      two back out; continue to work in and out, in and out,
      etc.
   b. *All* walk in, all walk out.
   c. All hold tube above heads; turn inside out.
   d. Travel in a circle; walk, skip, run, hop, etc.
   e. Sit with legs straight, feet together; one and three lie
      down, two and four sit up; alternate up and down.
   Try other combinations with small group work. Make up
new ideas and have the students create new activities.

Note: Be sure to *tape* down the valve of the inner tube so that it
   does not protrude and become a safety hazard.

Wooden Blocks

Acquisition

   Wooden blocks of varying sizes can be acquired at lumber
yards by asking for scrap pieces from cuttings. Carpenters on
building jobs are often willing to part with scrap pieces.

Construction

   Wooden blocks for movement exploration activities should be
approximately 5 inches by 12 inches to 14 inches by 5 inches.
They can be sanded and painted in a variety of bright colors.

Objectives

   To help children develop balance skills.

   To help children develop spatial awareness.

   To help children develop locomotor skills.

Activities with wooden blocks

1. Stand the blocks on end and try hopping and jumping over
   them.

2. Place wands across two blocks and find various ways to get
   over and under the wands.

Wooden blocks can be used for hurdles.

3. Stand on the end of the block and balance on one foot; then on the other.

4. Place the block on its side and balance on the side.

5. Stand several blocks on end and use for obstacle course or relays.

6. Use the blocks for game markers.

7. Use the blocks for target toss or bowling pin knock-down.

Foot Launchers

Acquisition

For each foot launcher purchase a piece of lumber 3 feet in length. Use some scrap wood to create a 1- by 6-inch fulcrum 2 inches tall.

Construction

Nail the fulcrum 6 inches from one end of the 3-foot board as seen in the picture. The board can be painted with a foot at the short end and a beanbag at the long end to give the child a visual cue.

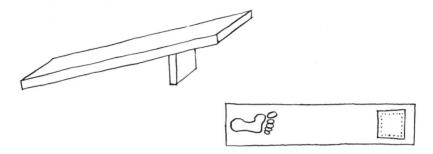

Foot launchers help develop eye-hand and eye-foot coordination.

Objectives

To develop eye-hand, eye-foot, and gross-motor coordination.

To increase a child's self-concept and spatial awareness.

Activities

1. Place a beanbag on the end of the board. Have the child stand on the raised end of the board to launch the beanbag. Then have the child try to catch the beanbag while it is in the air.

2. Vary the launched object such as yarn ball, fleece ball, and paper ball.

3. Have the child attempt to launch the object to specific height, such as his waist, chest, chin, eyes, etc.

4. Have the child attempt to catch the objects with different body parts such as his palm, back of hand, wrist, elbow, and foot.

CHAPTER 4

Low-Cost Equipment

Alphabet and Number Beanbags

Acquisition

Use old scraps of material or felt and dried peas, navy beans, or styrofoam balls from old beanbag chairs.

Construction

Cut the material into the shapes of the numbers or letters, sew the forms together with strong thread until only a small hole remains, fill with beans, and complete the sewing. Many times a project such as this can be carried out by the home economics classes in the schools or by volunteer parents.

Objectives

To help children learn to distinguish numbers and letters.

To manipulate and investigate an object.

To control an object so that creative and functional use is made of it.

To give an opportunity to explore the relationship of the object to the area around the child.

To develop fine-motor and eye-hand coordination.

Activities with beanbags

1. Letter and number recognition.
    a. Have the children spell their spelling words.
    b. Give the children their addition, subtraction, multiplication, and division tables and have them make the totals with beanbags.

Beanbags can be made into the shapes of numbers and letters.

   c. Throw the letter or number to various children and have them name the letter or number as they catch it.

2. Individual activities.
   a. Sit down, lie down, kneel, or close your eyes and do something with the beanbag.
   b. Place the beanbag on the floor and move around it or over it in several different ways.
   c. Move in space with the beanbag.
   d. Balance the beanbag on any part of your body as you move through space.
   e. Throw the beanbag up in the air while you move about the room.
   f. Throw the beanbag from one hand to another as you move about the room.
   g. Move the beanbag around your body as you change levels.
   h. Throw the beanbag into the air and use different parts of your body to catch it.
   i. Use various parts of your body to throw the beanbag into the air.
   j. Lie on your back and try to throw the beanbag into the air and catch it.
   k. Place the beanbag on the floor and build different types of bridges over it with your body. Make the bridges with three, four, five, or six body parts touching the floor.
   l. Place the beanbag on the floor and move it with different body parts. Try your elbow, knee, heel, or head.

3. Partner activities.
   a. Find a partner and exchange beanbags on the floor.
   b. Find several different ways to exchange beanbags in the air.
   c. Exchange beanbags with a partner using body parts other than your hands.
   d. Move about the room with a partner and exchange beanbags.

Beach Balls and Sponge Balls

Acquisition

Beach balls and sponges may be purchased inexpensively at local supermarkets, hardware stores, and department stores.

Construction

Beach balls and certain types of sponge balls such as "Nerf Balls" and ball items from Creative Playthings involve no construction. Round, oblong, or square sponges may be trimmed with a scissors and adapted for use in ball activities.

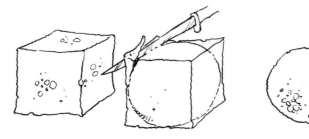

Balls can be made out of sponge.

Objectives

To develop creativity in the use of balls.

To develop fine-motor coordination.

To develop eye-foot and eye-hand coordination.

To develop familiarity with balls in a variety of situations.

To develop manipulative game-playing patterns and skills.

[1] Creative Playthings, Princeton, N.J. 08540.

Activities

The reader is referred to the section on ball-handling activities in chapter 2 (see page 9). Because beach balls and sponge balls are large, have a slow flight, and can be easily handled by young children, they are very adaptable to throwing, catching, and other manipulative activities. They may also be used for volleyball, basketball, and other sports which utilize balls.

Balloons

Acquisition

Any local toy store, department store, drug store, etc.

Construction

Large five-cent balloons work better than the oval or oblong variety. Use bread wrappers to fasten the balloons rather than tie them. Used in this manner, balloons can be deflated and used time and again.

Objectives

To develop manipulative movement patterns in children.

To develop eye-hand coordination, visual pursuit, and tracking patterns in children.

To develop finger tip or tactual control as a lead-up to ball-handling skills.

To develop body awareness, laterality, directionality, spatial relationships, and other perceptual-motor skills.

Activities with balloons

Various positions can be assumed while tapping the balloons into the air (lying down, sitting, kneeling, standing, etc.).
1. Singles.
   a. Tap the balloon into the air with one hand and then with the other hand.
   b. Tap the balloon into the air with one of your fingers. Now try some of your other fingers.
   c. Tap the balloon into the air with both of your hands.
   d. Tap the balloon quickly and rapidly and then slowly and gently.

e. Tap the balloon high into the air and then see how many times you can cross underneath the balloon before the balloon touches the ground.

f. Tap the balloon into the air with various parts of your body. Use your head, chin, shoulders, elbows, hips, feet, and knees. Use both sides of your body.

g. Put a penny or other similar weight inside the balloon and blow it up. How does the added weight change the flight pattern of the balloon as you tap it?

2. Partners.
   a. Volley the balloon with your partner using various body parts.
   b. Alternate right and left sides of your body as you pass the balloon to your partner.
   c. Use underhand taps and then overhead taps as you pass the balloon.
   d. Blow the balloon into the air to your partner.
   e. Tie the balloon on one of your ankles and walk, hop, or skip about the room as you try to step on and break other children's balloons. Last one to keep his balloon from being broken is the winner of the game.
   f. Papier-maché a balloon, decorate it, and play volleyball games which involve setting and volleying a ball.

Parachutes

Acquisition

Parachutes can be purchased at: (1) surplus stores; (2) government surplus stores; (3) United Settlement, P.O. Box 907, Ansonia Station, New York, N.Y. 10023; (4) Educational Activities Inc., Freeport, Long Island, N.Y. Prices range from fifteen to thirty-five dollars and up.

Construction

There is no construction involved in the use of a parachute save for mending any holes you may find in the parachute. Parachutes with shroud lines are preferable because more activities are possible with lines attached to the chute.

Objectives

To provide a good workout for the muscles of the upper body.

To learn team cooperation and its necessity for success.

To develop rhythmical qualities in children.

Activities with the parachute

1. Activities with shroud lines.
    a. Straddle rope walking in to the parachute, turn, straddle out.
    b. Criss-cross feet over line, one foot, then the other.
    c. Hop on two feet from one side of the line to the other.
    d. Balance as you walk on the line forward, backward, and sideways.
    e. Perform the activities *a* through *d* with the line in a curved position.
    f. Hop over the shroud lines all the way around the parachute.
    g. Skip or run over the shroud lines all the way around the parachute.
    h. Sitting with legs straight, pull in to the parachute.
    i. Lie flat on your back with your feet toward the center and pull up to a sitting position; then back to the floor gently.
    j. Lie on your stomach and pull in to the parachute.
    k. Holding the rope to your waist, turn in to the parachute winding the rope around your waist—*not* legs.
    l. Snap the lines on the floor to the rhythm of the music.
    m. Children at the even-numbered spots jump rope with their shroud lines.

2. Activities with the chute.
    a. *Waves:* Holding on to the parachute with a firm grip, shake by raising your arms up and down.
    b. *Small Ripples:* Instead of moving your arms up and down together, move them in opposition, one hand up while the other is moving down.
    c. *Horse Pull:* With backs to parachute, grasp hands with palms up. On command "Pull," pull on parachute, hold, relax, and then change grip. Repeat. (Important, one foot is placed in front of the other for balance.)
    d. *Front Horse Pull:* Same as above, facing front. Emphasize arms straight or bent, depending on what is hoped to be accomplished.
    e. *Ring Around:* Holding on to parachute, all move in same direction by skipping, galloping, walking, running, or any

Parachutes encourage group cooperation.

other movement—waves can be made while doing this. Reverse direction.

f. *Popcorn:* Make waves while beach balls or sponge balls are being popped up in center of parachute.

g. *Raised Canopy:* Parachute on the floor. On signal "Up," parachute is raised up and held high (by moving in slightly on "Up" the parachute will go even higher, or children can get on tiptoes).

h. *Igloo:* On signal raise parachute up and then on "Down" bring to the floor (air is trapped inside). The class can stand on the band and be able to look over the parachute.

i. *Inside Igloo:* Children enjoy being inside the parachute. To execute, cross hands, turn around under the raised parachute, pull down over while lying or sitting down inside.

j. *Basket of Heads:* On knees, raise parachute as for igloo. On signal, lie down placing the parachute at the back of your neck with your head under the parachute and body outside, flat on the floor.

k. *Mushroom:* Grasping the chute with knuckles up, lower the chute to the floor. On command, all raise hands over heads and take one step forward. Take more steps for more height.

l. *The Mountain:* Grasping the chute with knuckles up, lower the chute to the floor. Place knees on edge of chute. Raise hands in air and allow chute to settle to the floor.

m. *Dance of the Strings:* Each child holds the edge of the parachute and throws his shroud line into the center. Everyone shakes the parachute vigorously to make waves or make the strings dance to the rhythm of the music.

n. *Stepping Out:* With one child in the center of the parachute, make waves. Center child walks around the center picking up his feet higher than normal to step over the waves.

o. *Capture the Popcorn:* Put one child and a ball in the center and try to keep the child from catching the ball by making waves and playing Popcorn.

p. *Numbers In:* Have the children number off by fours or fives. Raise the parachute on signal and call one number. Those having that number go into the center and come back out to their own place when the chute starts to come down. Continue until all have been called.

q. *Numbers Change:* Same as above but change places with

someone as you come out. Anyone not getting a place is out of the game. Continue until all numbers are called. Different types of movement or locomotion can be specified for moving across the chute.

Hoops

Acquisition

While the commercial hoops are available in several sizes and a variety of colors, they are not nearly as well constructed as those which can easily be made from black plastic plumbing tubing for nearly half the price. The homemade hoops are more rigid, can be made without the use of staples, and the circumference can be made to meet any specific measurement. The plastic pipe or tubing and the couplers for joining the ends can be purchased at most hardware or the do-it-yourself handyman stores. Both pipe and the couplers are available in various sizes from ½-inch to 2-inch thicknesses. It is priced by the foot and according to size. Standard size hoops require 8 feet of ½-inch pipe and one ½-inch coupler. Approximate cost: $1.25.

Construction

Cut the ends of the tubing so that the ends will meet and join smoothly. Heat both ends of the pipe by dipping them in hot water. This enables the tubing to expand to allow the coupler to fit into the ends. Insert the coupler into the tubing and allow to cool.

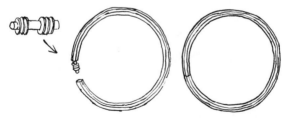

Hoops can be made from plumbing tubing.

Objectives

To allow for rhythmic development and timing in children.

To develop general coordination skills in children.

To teach children about form perception.

To develop body awareness, eye-hand coordination, spatial relationships, and other perceptual-motor skills.

Activities with hoops

Activities may be done alone, with a partner, with big hoops, and with little hoops.

1. Hoops are made for rolling.
    a. Roll the hoop, run ahead of it, catch it, and roll it back.
    b. Roll the hoop, and then run and hop, dive, or jump through it as it rolls along on the floor.
    c. Roll the hoop or spin the hoop in place and see how many times you can jump in and out of the hoop before it stops.
    d. How long can you keep the hoop rolling? How fast can you roll it? How slowly can you roll it? Can you roll the hoop and make it come back to you?
    e. Can you roll the hoop with some part of your body besides your hands? Can you keep the hoop rolling by using a stick?
    f. Can you bounce a ball through the hoop while it is rolling? How many times can you pass a ball back and forth to your partner before the hoop stops rolling?

2. Hoops are made for throwing and catching.
    a. Toss the hoop into the air and catch it.
    b. Toss the hoop in the air so that it comes down horizontally with you in the center.
    c. Toss the hoop from a low position. Jump to a high position and catch it.
    d. Toss the hoop up high in the air and turn around before you catch it.
    e. Using two or more hoops, try to juggle them.

3. Hoops are made for rotating.
    a. Rotate the hoop around various body parts—wrists, arms, neck, legs, ankles, hips, or waist. Can you keep more than one hoop going at a time?
    b. Can you walk, run, skip, hop, or gallop while you keep the hoop rotating around you?
    c. Can you walk across a balance beam while rotating the hoop?
    d. Can you keep the hoop rotating while your body assumes different poses?
    e. Can you bounce a ball or jump while you keep the hoop rotating around you?

4. Hoops are made for self-testing and gymnastics activities.
   a. Can you jump rope with a hoop?
   b. Can you start the hoop at your neck, and twirl the hoop down to your feet and back up to your neck?
   c. Can you do a cartwheel by placing your hands in the middle of the hoop?
   d. Can you do a handspring by placing your hands in the middle of the hoop?
   e. Crawl through the hoop using various body positions, levels, and bases of support.
   f. Do tumbling stunts with hoop and partner. For example, perform a dive roll through a vertical hoop held by a partner.

5. Hoops are made for rhythmical and game activities.
   a. Any of the rolling, throwing, tossing, or rotating activities lend themselves to a variety of relay games and races.
   b. Place twenty to forty hoops on the floor in a pattern. This makes an excellent maze for running, skipping, hopping, jumping, etc.
   c. Hoops can be used as targets for balls, beanbags, balloons, etc. They provide good stationary targets or moving targets as well.
   d. One or two children can hold a hoop horizontally while another jumps over and under or in and out. Also try to perform cart wheels through held hoops.
   e. Given one ball and one hoop, make up a game to play with one or two partners.
   f. Any music with a definite beat can be used for creating rhythmic movements. Records are. available with instructions for routines and exercises. What can you do with your hoop to keep in time with the beat of the music?

Batting Tees

Acquisition

Batting tees may be constructed from a variety of objects found in the environment. Construction or traffic cones, radiator or water hoses, dowels, plastic tubing, and wiffle bats are among the materials that can be used. Find the materials available to you and adapt them to make them work in your situation.

Construction

Batting tees can be made in different ways. One way to make one is to cut out the top end of a wiffle ball bat and then slip the bat through the end of a traffic cone as seen in the picture. To make a wooden tee, obtain a piece of 2- by 2-foot by 3/4-inch plywood to use as the base. Anchor a 1½- to 2-inch pole or dowel to the center of the base with nails or screws. The pole should be 2 to 3 feet tall depending on the size of the children with whom you are working. Attach a piece of hose such as a radiator water hose with an adjustable clamp to the pole. The hose can then be adjusted to the height of the children. Place the ball on top of the hose for the children to hit. The flexibility in the hose keeps the children from being jarred when they hit the ball.

Batting tees help children learn striking skills.

Objectives

To develop eye-hand coordination.

To develop concepts of laterality and directionality.

To develop gross-motor coordination.

Activities with batting tees

1. Use a table-tennis racket, paddle-ball racket, or wiffle bat and have the child hit a wiffle ball, yarn ball, or nerf (sponge) ball off the tee. As the child's skill increases, have him hit grounders or fly balls, or place his hits to right or left field.

2. Use a softball bat and a softball to perform the same activities as above.

3. Have a group of children play "Tee Ball." No pitcher is required. The rules are similar to softball or can be modified for any situation.

Target Loops

Acquisition

Two methods can be employed to develop a target loop for a variety of target games or activities. The first idea is to use the discarded base of a classroom globe (of the world). Most of the globes have a circular attachment at the top that can be used for the target. A second technique is to construct the target loop from a batting tee (see preceding section) and a hoop (see page 69).

Construction

If the globe base is used, no construction is necessary. If the batting tee and hoop are used, then the following method should be employed. Using the batting tee diagram from the previous section follow the same steps, except omit the radiator water hose from the structure. Instead of placing the rubber hose at the top of the tee, a small hole approximately 1 inch in diameter is drilled at the top of the tee. A homemade hoop (see hoop section) is then attached through the opening by attaching the ends of the hoop with a plastic coupler (see hoop section). See the picture below. A second way to attach the hoop would be to nail or staple the hoop to the top of the tee.

Objectives

To develop eye-hand coordination.

To develop throwing and catching skills.

To improve the child's depth perception.

Target loops help
children develop
eye-hand coordination.

Activities with target loops

1. Using the loop as a *target,* the children can work with some of
   the following ideas.
   a. Throw any type of ball through the target loop (sponge
      ball, yarn ball, playground ball, etc.).
   b. Work with a partner in throwing and catching different
      balls through the loops.
   c. Try to bat a balloon through the target loop.
   d. Toss a Frisbee through the target loop.
   e. Make up a game with two or more players, using one target
      loop and one ball.
   f. Use the target loop for developing accuracy with striking
      skills (paddles and tennis balls).
   g. Use target loop for developing sports skills, i.e., basketball
      passes, football passes, soccer kicks, etc.

Form Targets

Acquisition

Targets with simple geometric forms cut out or pictures
painted on the surface can be made from pieces of plywood or
cardboard boxes. Use discarded appliance boxes for large targets
or other boxes of varying sizes for different targets. Cardboard
boxes may be obtained for the asking from a variety of stores. Use
scraps of plywood or purchase 4- by 8-foot sheets of plywood
from a lumber store for wooden targets.

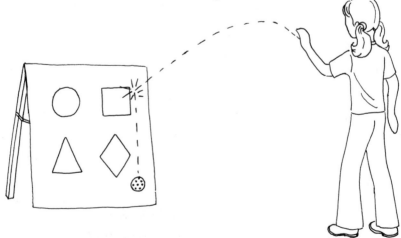

Form targets help children develop eye-hand coordination.

Construction

Cut holes in the boxes or plywood sheets by using simple geometric designs or cut holes in appropriate places such as eyes, nose and mouth from a picture which has been drawn on the target to be placed at various angles toward which the child can aim. The targets can be painted to create a more complete and attractive project.

Objectives

To help children develop eye-hand and gross-motor coordination.

To help children develop form perception.

To assist the child in learning how to plan motor activities.

To develop a child's tactile-kinesthetic perception.

Activities with form targets

1. Have the child stand at various distances from the target and try to throw objects such as beanbags through the holes.

2. Vary the angle of the target from perpendicular to the floor to parallel with the floor and have the child try to toss objects through the holes.

3. Tell the child to toss objects through specific holes in the target by aiming at specific geometric forms on command.

4. Have the child trace his/her fingers around the openings in the target to identify various forms.

Balance Puzzles

Acquisition

A set of magic markers and some sheets of 8½- by 11-inch paper, cardboard, or poster board are all that is needed for this project. You may already have these supplies at home or school, or they may be purchased at a local school-supply store.

Construction

The balance puzzles, as seen on the next page, can be made by drawing with a magic marker on the sheets of paper or by making charts with poster board or cardboard. The sheets or charts may be laminated for a more permanent product.

Code

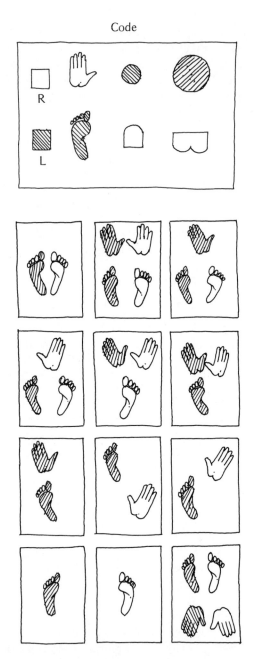

Balance puzzles help children develop static balance.

Objectives

To help children solve balance problems related to static balance.

To help children learn body awareness concepts.

To help children improve laterality and spatial orientation concepts.

To teach children better concepts of visual decoding, association, and memory.

Activities with balance puzzles

1. Starting with the easier puzzles, hold one chart up at a time and ask the child to balance on the body parts as shown in the puzzle. The child must balance with the correct parts (left or right) as well as in the same position as shown in the chart, with no other body parts touching the floor.

2. Use the puzzles as part of an obstacle course. When the children arrive at a puzzle they must perform the designated balance task before moving on to the next obstacle.

3. Show the child a chart and then remove it from his/her vision. Ask the child to assume the balance position through the use of visual memory.

4. Lay ten to twenty charts out on the floor and time the children to see how little time they can use to assume each of the positions as they progress from one chart to another in sequence.

5. Show the child two, three, or four charts and then remove them from his/her vision. Ask the child to perform each of the balance positions in sequence from memory.

Balance Boards and Balance Beams

Acquisition

Balance boards with 3-, 4-, and 5-inch bases can be made from 3/4-inch plywood with small pieces of 2- by 2-inch or 4- by 4-inch boards used as bases. Balance beams are constructed from 2- by 4-inch boards with small pieces of 2- by 4-inch boards and 1- by 2-inch boards acting as bases. All wood may be purchased from local lumber companies.

Construction

1. The top of the balance board is made by cutting a piece of 3/4-inch plywood into a 16-inch square. The bottom or base may be a 3-, 4-, or 5-inch square. To achieve proper dimensions on the base, glue and clamp 2- by 4-inch boards together and allow time to dry. Then cut to appropriate size. Countersink wood screws or nails to attach the top to the base.

2. The walking surface of the balance beam may be a 2- by 4-inch board of any length, preferably 8 to 12 feet. The base which

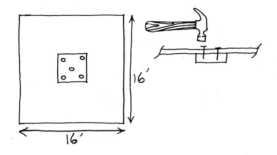

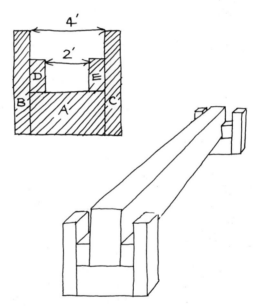

Balance boards and balance beams help children develop balance skills.

holds the balance beam is constructed by cutting a piece of 2-by 4-inch board into three pieces 4 inches in length and attaching them as shown in the picture (A, B, C). Two 1- by 1-by 2-inch boards are attached to the inside of the base as shown in the picture (D, E). This allows the beam to be placed either on the 2-inch side or the 4-inch side.

Objectives

To teach children better stability and balance patterns.

To develop eye-foot coordination.

Activities with balance boards and balance beams

1. Balance boards.
   a. Balance on the board and touch different body parts including your knees, ankles, and toes.
   b. Touch various body parts with your eyes closed.
   c. Try to stand on your tiptoes with your eyes open and closed.
   d. Turn around while maintaining your balance on the board.
   e. Force yourself to lose your balance and then regain it while moving in a forward, backward, or sideways direction. Place your feet in different stride positions as you do this. What is the best position in which to place your feet as you tip in different directions?
   f. Bounce a ball while you balance on the board.
   g. Play catch with a partner as you balance on the board.
   h. Jump rope while you balance on the board.
   i. Assume different body positions with one, two, three, and four bases of support as you balance on the board.

2. Balance beam.
   a. Walk across the beam in forward, backward, or sideways directions.
   b. Use other forms of locomotion to get across the beam. Examples may be sliding, skipping, galloping, or hopping.
   c. Move across the beam with different bases of support including one, two, three, and four bases.
   d. Move across the beam while balancing an object such as an eraser on different body parts.
   e. Attempt to turn around while walking across the beam.
   f. Move across the beam and step over or under a wand placed at various heights along the beam.
   g. Stand on the floor and hop or jump from one side of the beam to the other. Hop and jump in forward, backward, and sideways directions.
   h. Walk on the floor and place feet on alternating sides of the beam. Place the right foot on the left side of the beam and the left foot on the right side of the beam.
   i. Roll a ball across the beam.
   j. Bounce or dribble a ball as you walk across the beam.
   k. Play catch with a partner as you walk across the beam.
   l. Exchange places with a partner as you walk across the beam.

Springboards

Acquisition

For each springboard purchase a wooden board approximately 10 feet by 8 inches by 1 inch and two cement blocks at a local lumber company. In some instances local builders may be willing to donate the materials.

Construction

Sand or file all of the rough edges off the board. You may also wish to paint the board and blocks. No further construction is necessary. Place the board on the blocks in a horizontal position with a slight overlap at the edges to give added support.

Objectives

To develop greater balancing skills.

To improve gross-motor coordination.

To increase spatial awareness.

To help overcome earthbound problems.

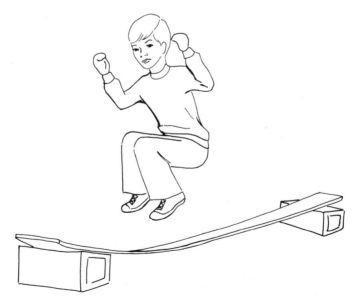

Jumping on a springboard helps develop coordination skills.

Activities with springboards

1. Have the child stand in the center of the board with his feet together. Have him jump in place several times, increasing the height he can jump as he increases in skill.

2. Have the child step on and off the board several consecutive times. He can do this forward, backward, and to each side.

3. Tell the child to jump on the board a specific number of times and then to stop. Teach the child to bend his knees, ankles, and hips to absorb the force in order to stop.

4. Use the board as part of an obstacle course. For example, crawl under, jump over, walk across, and hop on the spring-board.

For additional ideas refer to the balance beam and balance board activities in the preceding section.

Rocker Boards

Acquisition

A 1- by 6-inch by 3-foot board is needed for each rocker board. In addition, about 7 feet of 1- by 1-inch trim is necessary for use as a track or guide along with a 2- to 5-inch cylinder to be used as the support or fulcrum for the rocker board. Materials can be obtained from lumber scraps at construction sites or purchased at a local lumber company.

Construction

On the bottom of the 1- by 6-inch by 3-foot board attach the 1- by 1-inch trim, as in the picture on the next page. This provides a track along which the board may be guided. Cut the cylinder so that it fits just inside the track.

Objectives

To help children learn static balance concepts.

To help children develop better concepts of laterality, directionality, and spatial awareness.

To help children cross the midline of their bodies.

Children can balance on the rocker boards.

Activities with rocker boards

1. Have the child roll from side to side and touch the right and left ends to the floor alternately while maintaining control of his/her body. Have the child use his/her arms for more control.

2. Have the child try to maintain balance in the middle without either end touching the floor for as long as possible.

3. Have the child cross his/her legs so that the right leg will be forced to balance on the left side and vice versa.

4. Have the child bounce a ball or perform various visual pursuit tasks while balancing on the rocker board.

Stilts

Acquisition

One 2- by 4-inch by 8-foot pine or yellow poplar board should be purchased from a local lumber company for each set of stilts desired.

Construction

Cut 12 inches off the end of the 8-foot board. Cut the 12-inch board in half. Take the 6-inch board and cut it diagonally in half to make steps as illustrated in the picture. Cut the remaining 7-foot board lengthwise to make two 2- by 2-inch poles. Nail or bolt the steps to the poles as illustrated in the picture. Put rubber caps on the bottom of the poles to prevent slipping or damage to the floor.

Objectives

To develop better balancing skills.

To develop better eye-hand and eye-foot coordination skills.

To develop an awareness of laterality, directionality, and spatial awareness.

Activities with stilts

1. Methods of getting on the stilts.
   a. Lay the stilts on the floor. Stand at the top of the stilts. Pick up the stilts and place them under the armpits with the arms around the front of the poles. Place one foot on one of the steps, push up with the free leg, and place the free leg on the step of the second stilt.
   b. Hold on to the stilts as in the above procedures. Mount the stilts from an elevated position such as a chair.

2. Walk forward, backwards, and sideways with the stilts.

3. Create an obstacle course. Give students an opportunity to step over, under, around, and through objects.

4. Place hands on the top of the stilts and walk.

5. Try to jump or hop while on the stilts.

6. Try to walk up steps while on the stilts.

7. Stand on one stilt, lift the other leg up, and swing it around.

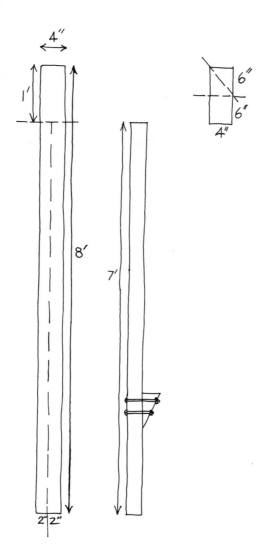

Stilts can be constructed from scrap lumber.

Jump Ropes, Elastic Ropes, and Chinese Jump Ropes

Acquisition

Sash cord in 3/8- to 5/8-inch size may be purchased in 100-foot hanks in local hardware stores. Elastic ropes or cord may be purchased in local department or sporting goods stores in any desired length. Chinese ropes are made from rubber bands.

Construction

1. Short jump ropes should be cut in 8-foot lengths or long enough so that the ends reach the armpits when the child is standing in the middle of the rope on the floor. Long jump ropes should be cut in 16-foot lengths. Tie the ends, tape the ends, or dip in hot wax to prevent unraveling.

2. There is no construction involved in making elastic ropes except for cutting the elastic in various lengths for individual, partner, and group activities. The ends of the elastic may be attached together by tying or sewing to make a loop for selected activities.

3. Chinese jump ropes are made by looping rubber bands together in chain fashion until the desired length is achieved. Use heavy rubber bands for best results.

Objectives

To develop agility, muscular coordination, and endurance in children.

To develop eye-hand and eye-foot coordination.

To develop rhythmical awareness and a better sense of timing in children.

To make creative use of ropes through forming geometric shapes, letters, and numbers.

Activities with jump ropes, elastic ropes, and Chinese jump ropes

1. Short jump rope.
   a. Place the rope on the floor in a long line and walk along it in as many ways as possible using one, two, three, and four bases for support.
   b. Form the rope into different letters of the alphabet by using different body parts such as feet, elbows, or hands.

Elastic Cord

Rubber Band Chain
(Chinese Jump Rope)

Examples of how elastic cord and rubber bands can be used.

    c. Jump or hop from one side of the rope to the other in forward, backwards, and sideways directions.

    d. Form the rope into different numbers by solving simple addition, subtraction, multiplication, or division problems.

    e. Turn the rope forward and try different methods of jumping—rebound jump, jump on one foot, alternate feet when jumping, jump in place, progress forward in a run, etc.

    f. Turn the rope backwards and try the methods of jumping above.

    g. Turn the rope to one side of the body or from one side to the other in figure-eight fashion while jumping in place to the rhythm of the turn.

    h. Experiment with time while jumping, first jumping slow and then fast.

2. Long jump rope.

    a. With partners holding the rope at different levels, try to jump over as in high jumping.

    b. With partners cradling the rope from side to side, try to jump the rope.

    c. Try rebound jumping while the partners turn the rope at various speeds.

    d. Try to go in the "front door" and "back door" while the rope is turning.

    e. With four turners at four corners, try to jump the double rope.

    f. Try to jump the long rope while you try to jump a short rope which you turn yourself.

    g. With two turners and two long ropes, try to jump "double Dutch" as the ropes turn in opposite directions.

3. Elastic ropes.

    a. Stretch the rope at different levels and try to jump over or slide under the rope as you move across the floor.

    b. Move over and under the rope in as many ways as you can while using different bases of support.

    c. Use the elastic rope as an opposing force for stretching exercises.

    d. Create different geometric shapes with the individual, partner, or group rope by stretching the rope in different directions. Use different parts of the body to stretch the rope.

4. Chinese jump ropes.
   a. Use for single or double rope jumping.
   b. Use as an opposing force for stretching exercises.
   c. Create different geometric shapes by stretching the rope in different directions. Stretch the rope with the hands and arms or do various hopping or jumping patterns to create the shapes.

Scooter Boards

Acquisition

One 12- by 12- by 3/4-inch piece of plywood with two good sides and four good quality casters with rubber wheels are needed for each scooter board.

Construction

Round off the corners of each piece of 12- by 12-inch plywood. Sand the edges so that they are smooth. Mount one caster on each of the four corners with wood screws. Drill a 1-inch hole in the center of the scooters so that they may be stored vertically by placing them on a dowel one by one.

Objectives

To develop upper arm and trunk strength in children.

To develop the ability of children to cooperate with a partner.

Activities with scooter boards
1. Individual activities.
   a. Kneel on the scooter board and push yourself around the gymnasium or obstacle course with your arms.

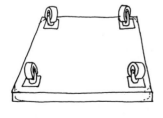 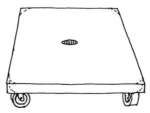

Scooters can be constructed from plywood and swivel wheels.

    b. Lie down on your stomach on the scooter board and push yourself around the room with your arms.

    c. Sit down on the scooter board and push yourself around the room with your legs.

    d. Utilize the above activities in relays.

    e. Modify the games of basketball, soccer, or other games by using the scooters as the source of locomotion.

2. Partner activities.

    a. While one child sits or kneels on the scooter, have a partner push him about the room or through an obstacle course by placing his hands on the shoulders of the child sitting down and pushing from behind.

    b. Allow one child to pull another about the room by having one child hold tightly to the ends of a jump rope as he sits on the scooter and by having a partner put the middle of the rope around his waist while he runs around the room.

    c. Perform the above activities in relays.

Towels

Acquisition

Old towels from home or the school laundry system may be used as pinnies (see picture), flags, or beaters. Velcro fastener material may be purchased from a local fabric shop.

Construction

When used as pinnies, the towels should be dyed various colors to designate teams. A hole should be cut in the middle of the towel so that it may be worn in poncho style as in the picture. Velcro fasteners should be sewn to each side of the towel so that it fits snugly to the body. When used as flags, the towels should be cut in strips. When used as beaters, the towels should be folded in half and taped in several spots to hold the sides together.

Objectives

To allow for differentiation of teams or squads in the various physical education activities involving games or rhythms.

To create an object which may be used as a flag in games such as Flag Football.

To create an object which may be used as a striking implement in games such as Beater Goes Round.

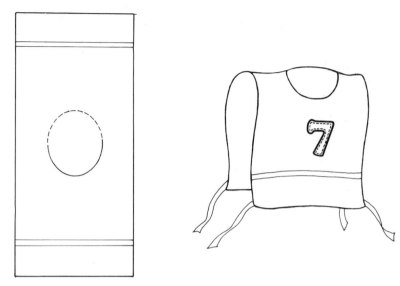

Towels can be used to make pinnies.

Activities with towels

1. Pinnies may be worn in any type of movement activity in which teams are designated.

2. Flags may be tucked into the gym trunks or under a belt and used in games such as Flag Football.

3. Towels may be loosely wrapped and used as striking implements in games such as Beater Goes Round. The softness of the towels will prevent injuries from being struck too hard.

Jumping Boxes

Acquisition

Various size jumping boxes can be made from 3/4-inch plywood which can be purchased from local lumber companies. Beer cases or similar strong cardboard boxes also make fine jumping boxes.

Construction

Boxes of 8, 16, and 24 inches in height should be constructed to provide movement experiences for children at different levels of complexity. To make a box 8 inches in height, nail four 8- by

16-inch pieces of plywood together to form the sides and nail a 16-inch square on top. To make a box 16 inches in height, nail four 16- by 16-inch pieces of plywood together to form the sides and nail a 16-inch square on top. To make a box 24 inches in height, nail four 24- by 24-inch pieces of plywood together to form the sides and nail a 24-inch square on top. To provide for these exact dimensions, cut each board with a 45° angle and make the outer diameters of the boards the above dimensions. For stronger support, nail braces on the inside of the boxes. Strong cardboard boxes involve no construction except for possibly painting them bright colors.

Objectives

To help children develop better locomotor movement patterns of jumping.

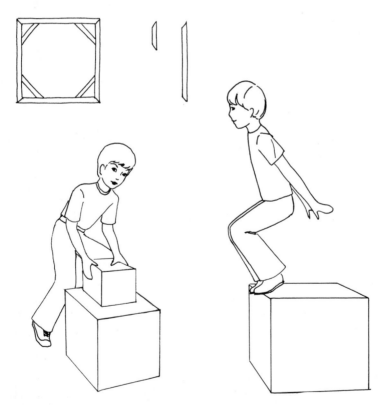

Plywood can be used to construct jumping boxes.

To help children learn how to absorb the force of their bodies when landing from a jump.

To allow children a chance for creative movement expression through the exploration of space.

Activities with jumping boxes

Go to a box and see how many ways you can get on and off the box.

a. Keep finding different ways to get on the box, but now try to fly off and land on your feet.

b. Get on the box and try to create different stretch and curl shapes using different bases of support.

c. Try to create different stretch and curl shapes in the air as you fly off the box.

d. As you land, absorb the force of your body by bending at the ankles, knees, and hips.

e. As you land from your flight off the box perform a roll by bending your various body parts.

f. Get on the box and make a shape. Hold the shape for five counts. Fly off the box and make the same shape in the air.

g. Move about the room and see how many ways you can get over the boxes as you come to them.

h. Experiment with levels as you move on and off the boxes. For example, get on the box with your body at a high level and get off the box with your body at a low level.

Parallettes and Low Parallel Bars

Acquisition

Two 3-foot lengths of 2- by 4-inch boards and two 12-inch lengths of 2-inch diameter wooden handrail are needed for construction of the parallettes. One 3- by 4-foot by 3/4-inch piece of plywood, four 12-inch lengths of 4- by 4-inch board, and two 4-foot lengths of 2-inch diameter wooden handrail are needed for construction of the low parallel bars. "L" braces are suggested as supports for the low parallel bars. Wood screws are needed for the construction of both pieces of equipment. All materials may be purchased from a local lumber company.

Construction

1. Parallettes are made by connecting the pieces of wood together as shown in the picture. Make sure that the wood screws are countersunk so that they do not protrude above the surface. Fill the countersunk holes with plastic wood and sand smooth. A wooden ladder may also be cut into 3-foot lengths and used by utilizing the rungs of the ladder as the grips.

2. When constructing the low parallel bars, mark an inside rectangle that is 8 inches from the outside edge of the plywood. Place one length of 4- by 4-inch board at each corner of the marked off rectangle. Secure the 4- by 4-inch board to the plywood by inserting the wood screws underneath the plywood up into the 4- by 4-inch board. Use three screws for each 4- by 4-inch board. Reinforce each 4- by 4-inch board with one or two "L" braces. Secure the handrails to the top of

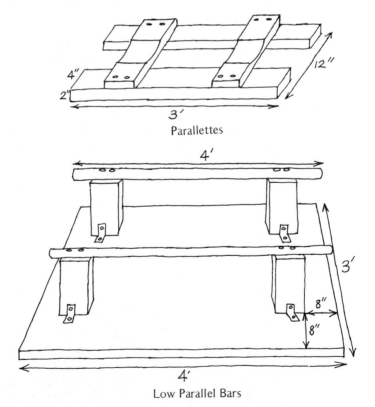

Parallettes

Low Parallel Bars

Parallettes and low parallel bars can be used for gymnastics.

the 4- by 4-inch board with wood screws. Be sure to counter-sink the screws so that they do not protrude above the surface of the handrail. Fill the holes with plastic wood and sand smooth.

Objectives

To develop upper body and arm strength.

To develop the ability to balance when in an inverted support position.

Activities with parallettes and low parallel bars

1. Place a mat underneath the parallettes and attempt to perform a tripod with the head on the mat and the hands on the bars.

2. Attempt to perform a "frog stand" on the bars.

3. With a partner in spotting position, try to perform a hand-stand. If necessary allow the partner to support the feet.

4. Mount the low parallel bars and assume a "crab" position. Allow a partner to perform several simple stunts such as a shoulder stand while using the first person as a base.

Peg Climbing Boards

Acquisition

Purchase the desired length of 2- by 10-inch hardwood board from the local lumber supply company. Dowels 1½ to 2 inches in diameter may also be purchased from the lumber company.

Construction

Drill holes in the hardwood board 1¾ to 2 inches in diameter about 6 inches apart in alternating fashion as illustrated in the picture. Boards may be mounted to the walls of the gymnasium in horizontal, vertical, or diagonal directions with ¼-inch or larger bolts and cement grommets. Dowels should be cut to be 6 to 8 inches in length.

Objectives

To develop upper body and arm strength.

To develop eye-hand coordination.

Activities with the peg board

1. Hanging activities.
   a. Insert one peg as high as you can reach and hang on it as long as you can using only one arm.
   b. Hang with two arms on one peg for as long as you can.
   c. Swing from side to side as you hang from two pegs.
   d. Do a flexed arm hang with your arms at a 90° angle.
   e. Perform as many pull-ups as you can.

Pegboards can be used for climbing.

2. Climbing activities.
   a. By swinging your body from side to side to establish momentum, climb up, down, sideways, or diagonally as many pegs as you can.
   b. Go "Around the World" by climbing from the first peg to the last peg and back to the start again.
   c. Try to climb up the peg board with your arms crossed.
   d. Place flags of countries by the peg holes and have contests to climb to the various countries (states could also be used).

Cargo Nets

Acquisition

Cargo nets are available from various equipment companies and army/navy surplus stores.

Construction

Attach the cargo net securely to the ceiling with appropriate clamps. Provide a system of pulleys to raise the net to the ceiling so that it is out of the way when not in use.

Objectives

To develop strength in the upper body muscles.

To improve agility and coordination in children.

To improve abilities in rope climbing.

Activities with the cargo nets

1. Individual activities.
   a. Climb on the net and see in how many directions you can move.
   b. See how many ways you can mount and dismount the net.
   c. Assume stretch and curl shapes while on the net by taking up as much and as little space as possible.
   d. Attempt to make geometric designs, body letters (alphabet), or body numbers while hanging on the net.
   e. Can you climb on the net using only your hands?
   f. Can you swing on the net or be swung?
   g. See how close you can get to another person on the net without touching.

Cargo nets can be used for climbing activities.

2. Group activities.
   a. Lower the net so that it is close to the floor. Assign one team of children to stand on each side of the net (with the front or back facing the net). On signal, each team tries to pull the opposing team over a line on the floor.
   b. Play tag while climbing around on the net.
   c. Play the game of "Twister" on the net by placing different color strips of cloth on the net.
   d. Perform various relay activities using the net.[2, 3]

[2]Bellardini, H. E., "A Sampling of Activities for the Cargo Net," *Journal of Health, Physical Education, and Recreation* 41:32-3, January, 1970.
[3]Hichwa, J. S., "The Cargo Net," *Journal of Health, Physical Education, and Recreation* 41:30-1, January, 1970.

CHAPTER 5

Gymnasium Ideas

Bases: Tile and Carpet Samples

Acquisition

Pieces of tile can be obtained from carpet or tile stores or from leftover materials on building sites. Carpet samples can be obtained from the same sources.

Construction

The tile or carpet samples should be in 8- or 10-inch squares. They can be trimmed to a variety of sizes.

Objectives

To help students in the development of running, hopping, jumping, or stepping skills.

To help students in the development of spatial awareness.

Activities with tile or carpet samples

1. Use the tiles or carpets for bases in kickball, long base, softball, hit pin baseball, and other base-type games.

2. Use the tiles or carpets for all types of tag games.

3. Use the tiles or carpets for stepping stones, hopping, jumping, or stepping from base to base.

4. Use the tiles or carpets as targets for beanbag toss.

Charts: Window Shades for Task Cards, Tumbling Sequences, Fitness Stations

Acquisition

Vinyl window shades can be obtained from most households or can be purchased at low cost from discount or hardware stores.

Other materials, such as poster board, styrofoam sheets, light plywood, and other inexpensive building sheets can be used for charts. Many of these can be made from scrap material or purchased at low cost.

Construction

The window shades can be used in their original form, even though they come in a variety of sizes. Felt marking pens or other types of ink can be used for the drawings or directions. Window shade brackets or other hanging devices should be mounted on the gymnasium wall so that the shades can be placed in a semipermanent fashion.

The other materials can be cut to a standard size (2 by 3 feet is a workable dimension) and stored in stacks or on shelving. A variety of methods can be used to print the skills or tasks on the posters. Felt markers, ink, crayon, and other methods are suitable.

All printing should be in large letters and on a vocabulary level suitable for the ages of the children.

Window Shades   Fitness Charts

Window shades and charts can be used for individualized instruction.

Objectives

To assist pupils in the development of a variety of skills, depending on the particular chart being used.

To facilitate learning by using a number of teaching stations at one time.

To correlate physical education tasks with reading and visual pursuit.

To facilitate the individualization of instruction in a variety of activities.

To help pupils develop overall physical fitness.

Activities with charts

1. Use the charts in the development of skill progressions for the following activities.
   a. Rope skipping.
   b. Balance beam.
   c. Ball handling.
   d. Hoops.
   e. Bike inner tubes.
   f. Tumbling
   g. Trampoline.
   h. Rope climbing.
   i. Vaulting.
   j. Any task where apparatus (small or large) is being used.

2. Use the charts in developing physical fitness stations for circuit training. Examples of the physical fitness stations would be sit-ups, pull-ups, squat thrusts, jumping jacks, windmill, bench step, and others. A variety of exercises could be used at each station.

Equipment Storage: Barrels, Cardboard Boxes, Large Bread Boxes, Cupboards, Other

Acquisition

Materials to be used for the storage of equipment can be found in many places. Many of these items are inexpensive and usually last for a long periods of time. Below are suggested sources.

Cardboard boxes: grocery stores, other retail stores.

Cardboard soap barrels: can be obtained from soap powder companies or from institutions, such as schools, hospitals, or large business firms.

Plastic custodial barrels (on wheels): can be obtained from schools, hospitals, and other institutions when they are finished using them. They could also be purchased commercially.

Wooden cupboards or shelving: can be made with inexpensive lumber or could be purchased commercially.

Large plastic bread or vegetable containers: large retail supermarkets use these for distributing bread, vegetables, and fruit. These could be donated to the schools or sold at a low cost.

Other: a variety of storage needs can be met by fitting the storage technique to the type of equipment being stored.

Construction

Cardboard boxes should be approximately 12 by 24 by 12 inches deep, but this can vary with the type of equipment. Standardizing the size of the boxes helps with shelf space and neatness.

Cardboard soap barrels are usually standard in size. They could be painted or decorated in a colorful manner.

Large plastic bread or vegetable containers need no construction.

Plastic custodial barrels need no construction unless for decoration purposes.

Wooden cupboards or shelving can be stained or painted. The shelving can be constructed in a variety of sizes and heights, depending on the space available and the storage needed.

Objectives

To provide the school with adequate storage for physical education equipment.

To encourage pupils to be neat and responsible in caring for equipment.

To facilitate learning and teaching.

Activities with storage items

1. Activities with the storage items are somewhat limited, although it is possible to use barrels for target toss and boxes for a variety of games or relays.

2. Activities will depend on the equipment that is being stored.

Note: All boxes, barrels, shelves, etc., should be marked and labeled with the name of the appropriate equipment appearing in large, bold letters. This will facilitate storage and save time.

High Jump Standards

Acquisition

Homemade high jump standards can be constructed from long pieces of 2- by 2-inch lumber, nails, and short pieces of 2- by 4-inch for bases. Scrap lumber or inexpensive pieces can be obtained at a lumber store.

Construction

The long pieces of 2- by 2-inch should be approximately 6 to 6½ feet in length. The short pieces of 2- by 4-inch should be used for cross bars at the base and should be approximately 2 feet in length. The long pieces can be nailed to the base. Starting at about 3 feet from the ground, graduated marks can be painted 1 inch apart. Nails with large heads can be angled into the column. Two of the standards should be made for high jumping. Bamboo poles or golf tubes telescoped together can be used for the cross bar.

Objectives

To help students to develop jumping skills.

To help students develop self-confidence through mastering a challenge.

Activities with high jump standards

1. Use the standards for high jumping.

2. Use the standards for obstacle courses (over or under).

3. Use the standards for developing perceptual-motor skills.

4. By using lower heights, the pupils can learn the limbo.

Hurdles: Tires, Wooden Blocks, Electric Conduit

Acquisition

Tires can be obtained at service stations or junkyards.

Wooden blocks can be made of scrap lumber or purchased at low cost from a lumber company. Old broom handles or golf tubes can be used for crossbars.

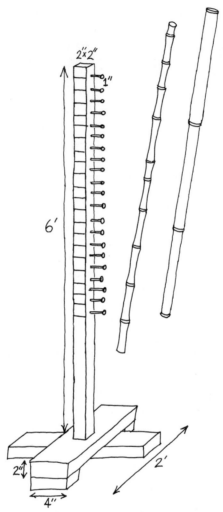

High jump standards can be made from wood scraps.

Electric conduit can be obtained at low cost from hardware or electric stores.

Construction

Tires can be set into the ground with two-thirds of the tire above ground. Set the tires so that they are equally spaced.

Wooden blocks: materials needed are two 36-inch lengths of 2- by 2-inch board, two 8-inch lengths of 2- by 6-inch board, and four 16-D common nails. The 36-inch lengths of lumber for the uprights of the hurdles can be notched for the desired jumping height. The uprights fit into a 2- by 2-inch notch cut into one side of the 8-inch length of 2- by 6-inch. This forms the base of the hurdle. Nails are then driven into the base of the hurdle. Old broom handles or golf tubes are the crossbars.

Electric conduit: This hurdle is formed from approximately 10 feet of 3/4-inch electrical conduit. The conduit is bent into the shape of the hurdle. The amount of material needed will depend on whether a 24-inch or 36-inch height is desired.

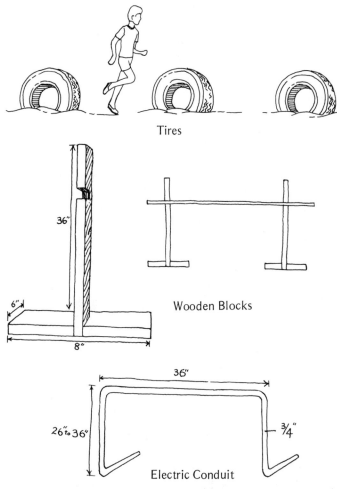

Tires

36"

6"

8"

Wooden Blocks

36"

26" to 36"

3/4"

Electric Conduit

Tires, wooden blocks, and electric conduit can be used for jumping experiences.

Objectives

To help students develop.track *skills,* especially as related to hurdling.

To present students with a challenge.

To help develop spatial awareness, flight, and landing patterns.

Activities with hurdles

1. Hurdles can be used for teaching track skills.

2. Hurdles can be used as part of an obstacle course (over and under).

3. Hurdles can be used as challenges in movement exploration (over, under, through, and around).

Jump-Reach Boards

Acquisition

A jump-reach board can be made of scrap chalkboard or of thin sheet metal. Chalkboard can be obtained from schools by asking administrators or custodians to save old portable chalkboards. A thin (1/8 inch thick or less) piece of sheet metal can be obtained at a junkyard or factory. Small magnets are needed for the metal board.

Construction

The chalkboard or sheet metal should be trimmed to approximately 24 to 30 inches in width and 48 to 60 inches in length. Felt markers or paint can be used to make 1-inch graduated markings on the board. Once the markings are completed the board should be fastened to a gymnasium wall with screws or bolts. Height should be determined by the age and size of the youngsters.

Objectives

To measure the students' leg power and jumping strength.

To provide the students with a challenge.

Activities with jump-reach board

1. The student stands beside the board, reaches up with one hand, and makes a mark with a chalk or attaches the magnet. From a standing position the student bends his knees, jumps

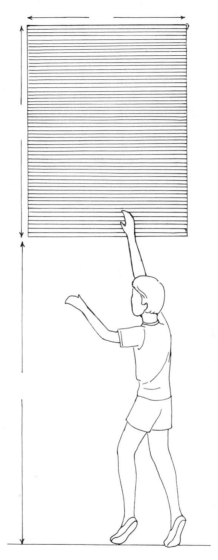

A jump reach board can be constructed from an old piece of chalkboard.

as high as he can, and makes a second mark (or places a second magnet) on the board. The difference is marked, and an indication of the student's leg power can be determined.

2. Use the jump-reach periodically to determine if increases are occurring in the student's power.

3. This activity is best suited for upper-grade students.

Marking Floor Areas

Acquisition

The substances used for marking gym floors, multi-purpose rooms, and other surfaces can be obtained in hardware stores, discount stores, art stores, and others. The type of surface and permanency desired will affect the choice of marking materials.

Construction

The following materials can be used for marking gym floors and other surface areas.
1. Paint (enamel).
2. Masking or pressure-sensitive tape.
3. White shoe polish.
4. Crayon.
5. Water-base tempera paint.
Use the above materials according to the directions.

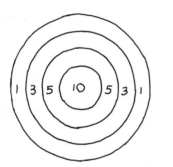
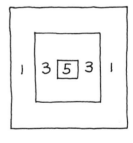

Wall and floor targets can be made from various substances.

Objectives

To correlate physical education activities with classroom activities (numbers, letters, shapes, geography, telling time).

To help in the development of motor skills.

Other objectives would be related to the specific activity developed with the marking.

Activities with markings

1. Games.
    a. Four-square.
    b. Hop-scotch.
    c. Wall-target games.
    d. Tic-tac-toe.
    e. Number and letter games.
    f. "Hop-the-Spots": using an irregular pattern of open and closed circles, ask the students to hop "left in the open, right in the closed" or to hop "one in the open, two in the closed." Place the circles about 8 to 12 inches apart but in a straight lane. (See chapter 6.)

2. Novelty activities.
    a. Paint large circles with the face of a clock. Use with time-telling games.
    b. Paint large circles by using geometric shapes for the outer edges, or alternate red and white marks to form the circle.
    c. Use numbers, letters, and colors in a variety of ways. (Stepping stones, hopping blocks, and geometric forms.) (See chaper 6.)
    d. Paint concentric circles on the walls for target and other games.
    e. Paint a map of the world on a large 4- to 6-foot cage or push-ball.
    f. Use varied colors for broad-jumping distances (as opposed to traditional feet and inches).
    g. Cut animal or human figurines from thin pegboard; paint and mount them on gym walls for decorative and game purposes.
    h. Use pegboard (painted with clown or pirate) in gym hallway to display lost-and-found items.

Nets for Team Sports: Clothesline, Sheets

Acquisition

Old clothesline can be obtained from most households or can be purchased at a hardware store. Sheets can also be obtained from households.

Construction

The clothesline can be used in a variety of lengths but preferably in the 30- to 40-foot category. This would allow for most net games. Smaller pieces can be used for smaller areas. The rope can be attached to any standards, to eye-hooks in the wall, or tied into the bleachers. Other types of fasteners could be used.

Strips of old sheets can be tied together to substitute for the rope. A whole sheet can be draped over the rope to add a new variation to the net games. With the sheet over the rope, the students must pick up the flight of the ball just as it passes over the top of the sheet.

Objective

To assist the students with the development of all of the necessary skills for badminton, volleyball, "net" ball, and other net sports.

Activities with nets

1. Use the ropes for "net" ball or Newcomb.

2. Use the ropes for volleyball.

3. Use the ropes for badminton.

4. Use the ropes for "balloon" ball (fine activity for primary and learning disability classes).

5. Use the ropes in the teaching of *any* net or related games.

6. Use the sheet over the rope as another variation to net games (see "Construction" above).

Old Mattresses

Acquisition

Old mattresses can usually be obtained from pupils in the school. Ask for used mattresses from home, but be sure they are clean and in reasonably good shape.

Construction

Again, make sure the mattresses are clean and free from any bad tears. Plastic covers could be made for the mattresses if needed.

Objectives

To help pupils develop techniques in landing.

To help pupils develop tumbling skills.

Activities with old mattresses

1. Use the mattresses as a "crash" or landing pad for vaulting activities (benches, vaulting horse, mini-tramp, vaulting box).

2. Use the mattress as a tumbling mat if no other mats are available.

3. Use the mattresses for protective landings when teaching the high jump.

4. Use the mattress under climbing ladders, balance beams, or climping ropes for protective padding.

5. Slope the mattress from an elevated surface and use for different kinds of rolling and turning.

Old Sheets

Acquisition

Old sheets can be obtained from almost any household. Students could bring the sheets from home.

Construction

A sheet can be used in its present form or cut into two large pieces. Use paint or magic markers in a variety of colors for marking the geometric shapes.

Objectives

To help children develop eye-hand coordination.

To help children develop spatial awareness.

To help children develop locomotor skills.

Activities with old sheets

1. Paint geometric shapes on the sheet; use a variety of sizes for triangles, squares, rectangles, circles, etc.

2. Children can hop, jump, walk, or leap from shape to shape as the sheet rests on the floor.

3. With the sheet resting on the floor, children can use beanbags for target toss (throwing at the various shapes).

4. Cut pieces of cardboard to conform to the painted shapes; mix the cardboard shapes and then ask children to match the cardboard shapes to the shapes on the sheet.

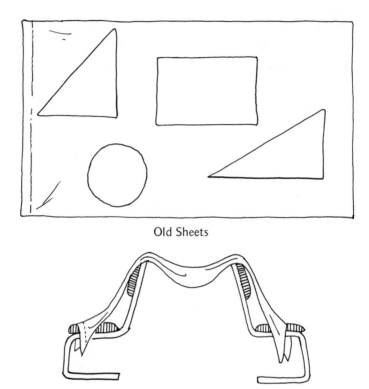

Old Sheets

Sheets can be used for many types of movement experiences.

5. Use the geometric designs to play a game of twister.

6. Have children stand around the edge of the sheet and as they grasp the edges, ask them to shake the sheet up and down (put lightweight balls in the center for a "popcorn" effect).

7. Use the sheet as a tunnel (over chairs or benches) for an obstacle course.

8. Have the children grasp the edges of the sheet and travel in a clockwise or counterclockwise motion, using various locomotor skills.

9. Paint letters or numbers on the sheet and make up similar games.

10. Be creative! See how many other games you can make up with the sheet.

CHAPTER 6

Adventure and Environmental Playgrounds

Structured Playgrounds

In our modern cities and urban areas city parks, recreation areas, and school playgrounds have been developed which are characterized by flat surfaces standardized into squares of sterility on which superstructures are erected to hang swings and stand slides, merry-go-rounds, and seesaws. The atmosphere of the play area and the realm of each piece of equipment are limited. Play areas are fenced in (or out) and pieces of equipment are placed in rows. Children are taught to play on each piece of equipment safely, which means essentially to sit down and get a free ride. The rules are all too familiar: *Don't* jump off a moving swing. *Don't* let go of the handles on a merry-go-round. *Don't* stand up and pump the swing. *Don't* get off the seesaw suddenly with your partner high in the air. *Don't* ride down the slide on your belly. *Don't* do this, *don't* do that. What movement challenges are left for children? In what creative role-playing experiences can children be involved?

The deficiencies of this type of playground as well as of the concrete jungle of streets and sidewalks are more clearly distinguished when contrasting the activities available to a child in a natural environment. In a natural setting the child can climb a tree, balance on a fence or railroad ties, jump from one stone to another in crossing a stream, throw stones, and dig in the earth. In nature, the child doesn't need devices, for he has a wealth of resources at his fingertips. The child doesn't consider any one spot as his playground. His playground is the whole world.

Alternatives

Fortunately, educators and others directly responsible for children's play experiences are beginning to recognize the deficiencies of the structured playground. In city or urban environments the trend is toward building environmental or adventure playgrounds.

This alternative approach to children's play areas is well founded on sound principles of equipment selection and construction and on the characteristics, needs, and interests of children. The following is a list of important principles for equipment selection and construction.

1. Equipment should be simple, natural, and inexpensive. Logs, telephone poles, automobile tires, cable spools, boxes, and the like are being substituted for commercial pieces which often cost thousands of dollars.

2. Equipment should be unlimiting and interpretive in use. Rather than using themes for playgrounds, use pieces of equipment which allow children to use their imagination and creativity to role-play.

3. Equipment should provide for large and small muscle development. Several pieces of equipment should be specially designed for the development of the muscles of the upper body, especially the shoulders and arms. Choose pieces of equipment with no movable parts so that children provide their own energy for physical development.

4. Equipment should provide for perceptual-motor development. Opportunities for balancing, locomotor skills, rhythmic action, manipulation, and space awareness should be available.

5. Equipment should be portable and/or adaptable. Selected play stations should be portable so as to be dismantled and reconstructed. Children enjoy change and variety. They like to carry and rearrange things to create their own play spaces.

6. Equipment should be attractive. Children like bright colors such as yellow, red, green, and blue. Avoid the use of gray, black, brown, and army green.

7. Equipment should be safe. Be aware of sharp edges, any protruding parts, and any weaknesses or flaws in materials. Make periodic checkups and replace any worn or damaged pieces of equipment.

A summary of some of the characteristics, needs, and interests of children at play illustrates agreement with the above principles.

1. Children like activities which allow them to balance.

2. Children like activities which provide for locomotor experiences such as running, jumping, climbing, and swinging.

3. Children like activities which allow for manipulative experiences such as throwing, catching, and kicking.

4. Children like to play in the soil. Sand boxes, piles of dirt, hills, leaves, and snow should be provided along with implements such as shovels, pails, rakes, and wheelbarrels.

5. Children like to play in the water. With all safety precautions taken, the water becomes a motivating place for children to play.

6. Children like to build. Lumber, hammers, nails, and saws should be provided so that children can build their own houses, forts, boats, and the like.

7. Children like to hide. They enjoy the feeling of being sought after and the anticipation of being found. Places should be provided which allow for the temporary safety from the seeking eyes of others.

8. Children like to pretend. They enjoy imitating and role-playing through various topics such as cowboys and cowgirls, astronauts, animals, machines, and family roles.

9. Children like adventure, thrills, and challenge. They enjoy being challenged physically, mentally, and emotionally. They like to take small risks and prove themselves successful in meeting them.

With these principles of equipment selection and construction and the characteristics, needs, and interests of children in mind, the remainder of the chapter provides ideas for building an environmental or adventure playground. The ideas have been divided into two categories of soft surfaces (grass, sand, dirt) and hard surfaces (blacktop and cement). Equipment ideas are suggested for the hard surface areas. Suggestions for activities are not indicated but should follow the concepts proposed above.

Soft Surface Equipment Ideas

Tires

Acquisition

Junkyards and service stations are very cooperative and willing to donate discarded bus, truck, and car tires. Make sure they are cleaned before put to use. If the tires wear out or are taken, they can always be replaced.

Construction

Joining.
Fastening.
Supporting.
Attaching to supports.

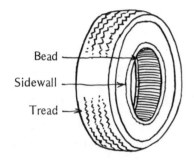
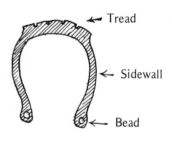

Joining tires: For construction purposes it is important to note that there are three basic parts of a tire: tread, sidewall, and bead.

Tread to Tread   Sidewall to Sidewall   Tread to Sidewall

Tires can be joined in three different combinations.

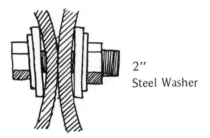

2"
Steel Washer

Fastening tires: Place a 3/8" x 2" cap screw through a 3/8" fender washer and a 3/4" steel washer. Then place this assembly through the drilled or punched holes in two tires, through a 3/4" steel washer, then a fender washer. Secure the joint by tightening on a 3/8" bolt.

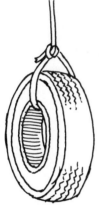

Supporting tires: Tying a rope around a tire is quick but the tire bead soon cuts the rope. A more durable joint can be made as follows: Cut a 12" length of 2" x 4" or 2" x 3" to the contour of the tire. Drill a hole through the center of the 2" x 4" and through the tire tread. Pass the rope through both and knot.

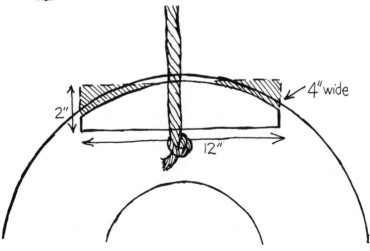

Attaching to supports: Ropes, chains, or cables can be attached to supports as shown below.

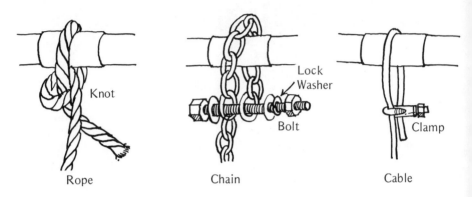

Rope   Chain   Cable

If the construction material is tight around the support, the first link acts as a pivot and wears out. If the construction material is loose around the support, the stress on it is relieved, but you will need to wrap it in a rubber sleeve (or shield with a piece of tire) to prevent the tree, pole, or pipe from wearing away.

Ideas for use

Use loose tires to sit on, relax in, roll, jump from, crawl through, pull, stack and hide in, run through, and play rockets, trains, boats, etc. Drill holes in the tires for drainage.

Use tires sunk in the ground for climbing, bouncing on, tunnels, designs, and mazes.

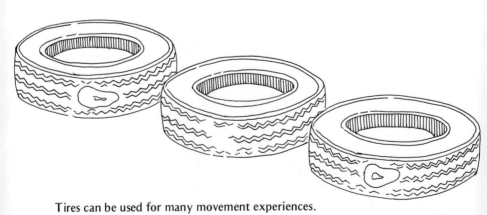

Tires can be used for many movement experiences.

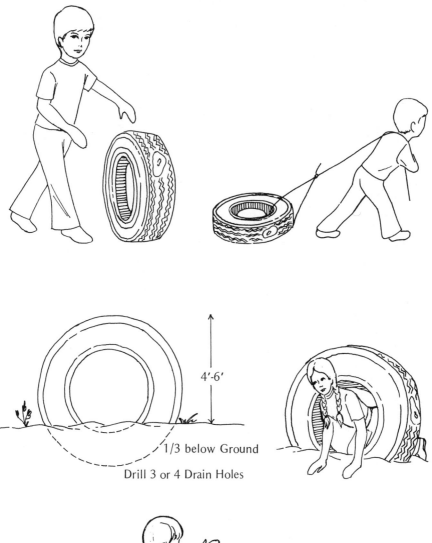

4'-6'

1/3 below Ground

Drill 3 or 4 Drain Holes

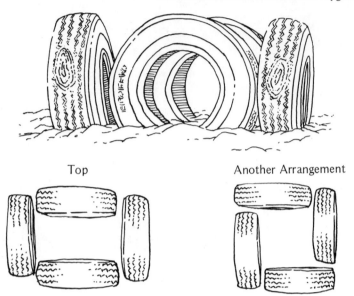

Top   Another Arrangement

Truck or bus tires can be bolted together to make a play house.

More elaborate arrangements make fun mazes. Tire mazes are particularly suitable for very young children.

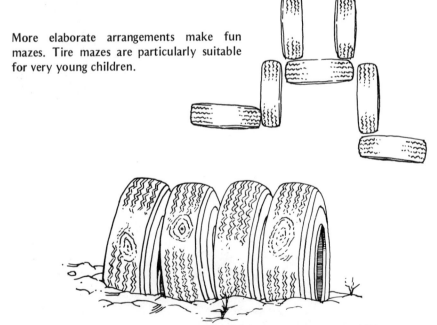

Tunnels should be kept short enough to allow adults to reach children.

Use tires with other equipment such as boards, poles, and rope to make balance apparatus, swings, ladders, slides, boats, climbing apparatus, and standards.

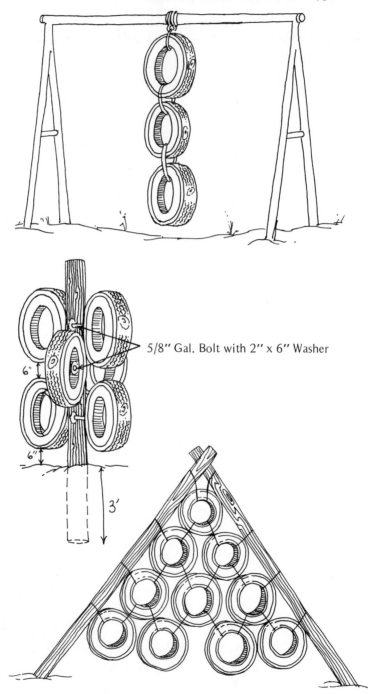

5/8" Gal. Bolt with 2" x 6" Washer

6"

6"

3'

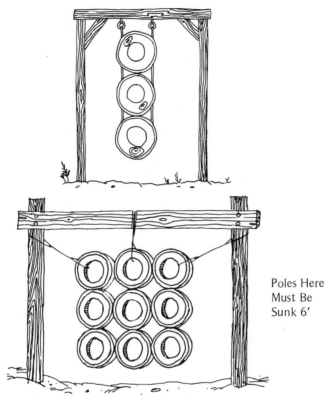

Each tire in the top row must be supported; otherwise it will bend and a child could fall.

Drain holes should be put in the bottom of each tire. Dirt and water will drain well from a 1" hole.

Front

At least a double row of tires must be used for stability. A single row will twist.

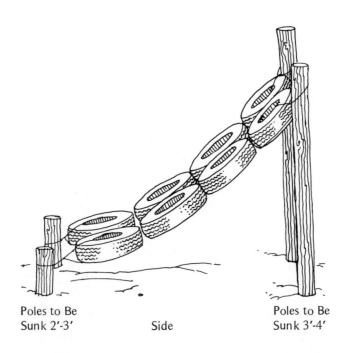

Poles to Be
Sunk 2'-3'   Side   Poles to Be
Sunk 3'-4'

Top View

Attach cable loops through poles and tires.

Poles Should Be
Sunk at Least 2'

A tire bridge should hang about 1' above the ground.

Use cement to anchor the poles to a tire base, then . . .

1. Connect two poles with a net or rope for school-age children to play games using balls.

2. Join two poles with a cord. From this hang a piece of cardboard for a beanbag pitching target.

3. Place parallel to fence. Stretch rope from fence to standards and back to fence. Cover for temporary shade or a play house.

4. Attach a tether ball to one pole and play a game.

Telephone Poles and Logs

Acquisition

Contact the local telephone and electric company for information regarding telephone poles. When informed about your project, they often provide used or replaced poles at a nominal cost. Logs can be obtained from trees which have been cut down.

Construction

Remove all dangerous splinters. Sink support poles into the ground 3 to 5 feet.

Ideas for use

Use poles sunk in the ground for balancing, climbing, and role-playing activities.

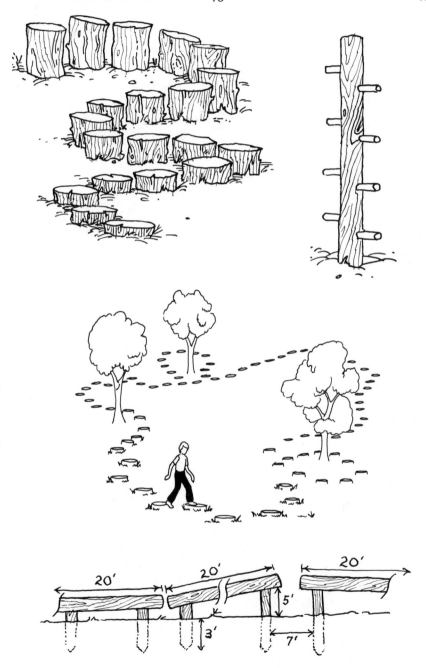

Telephone poles and logs can be used for many pieces of equipment.

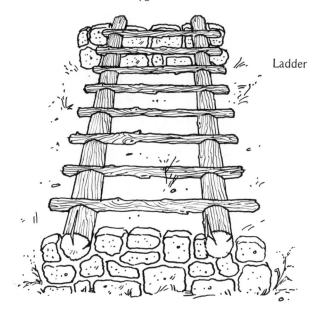

Ladder

Fort or Castle

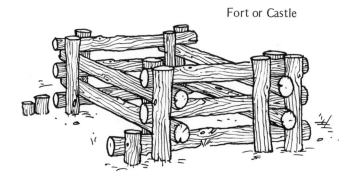

6' Square Minimum
8' Poles or Railroad Ties 8" Diam. Minimum
Sink Posts 2'
Horizontal Logs 6"-12" Diam., Varying Lengths

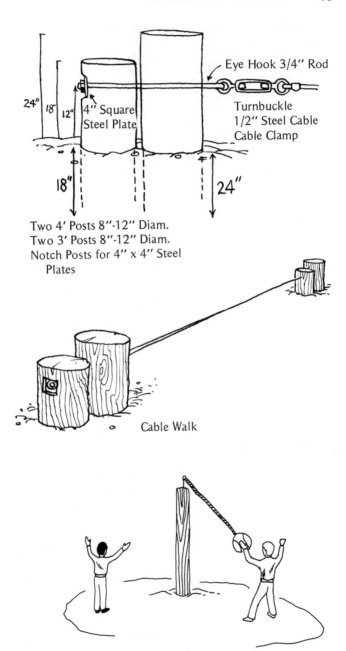

Eye Hook 3/4" Rod

24"   18"   12"   4" Square
                  Steel Plate

Turnbuckle
1/2" Steel Cable
Cable Clamp

18"   24"

Two 4' Posts 8"-12" Diam.
Two 3' Posts 8"-12" Diam.
Notch Posts for 4" x 4" Steel
    Plates

Cable Walk

Tether Ball

Poles with Cargo Nets

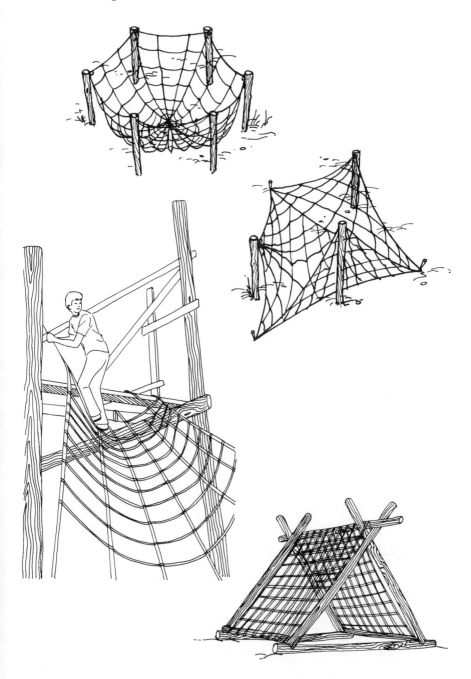

Cable Spools

Acquisition

Cable spools can be obtained from telephone and electric companies. When informed about your project, the companies will often donate them free of charge.

Construction

Remove all dangerous splinters. Paint the spools if you desire.

Ideas for use

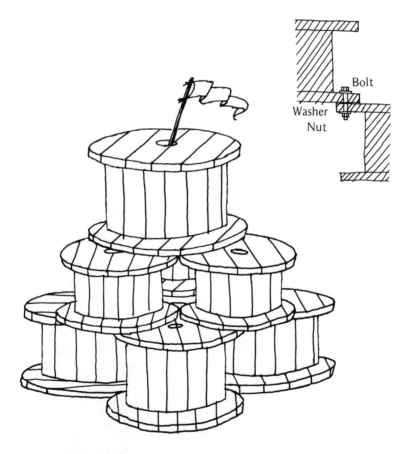

Cable Spool Castle

Cable spools can be used for many movement experiences.

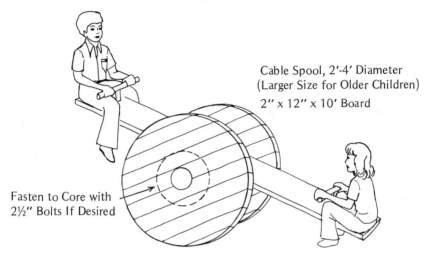

Cable Spool, 2'-4' Diameter
(Larger Size for Older Children)
2" x 12" x 10' Board

Fasten to Core with
2½" Bolts If Desired

Cable Spool Seesaw

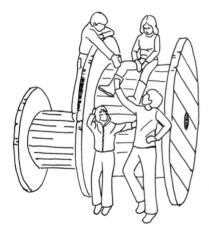

Spools for Climbing

Cable Spool Slide

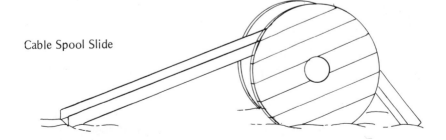

Sewer Tile

Acquisition

A large piece (or pieces) of sewer tile can usually be obtained from concrete plants that manufacture the tile. Some cost might be involved, although some companies might consider donating the tile to the school as a community service project. Building contractors might also be willing to part with a single piece of tile for the school playground.

Construction

The tile should be placed in a safe area of the playground. An effort should be made to secure the tile to the ground with large wood blocks, cement blocks, or other suitable anchors so that the tile cannot roll or move. The tile can be painted with a special cement paint.

Ideas for use

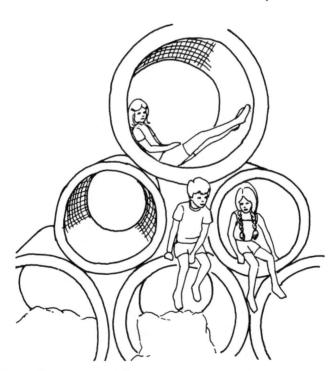

Sewer tiles can be used for several kinds of playground equipment.

A platform built on top of a sewer tile provides many play opportunities for children.

Children can provide their own art work on the tiles.

Building with Lumber

Acquisition

Purchase the lumber from a local dealer. A variety of sizes and lengths can be used. When the dealer is informed of the purpose of your project, he may give your school a discount price.

Construction

Saws, nails, bolts, hammers, wrenches, hole diggers, and paint will all be used for a project like this.

Ideas for use

Geometric Cubes

Platform with Slide

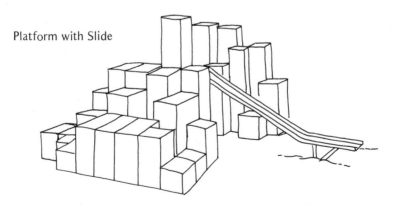

Lumber of all types and sizes can be used for playground equipment.

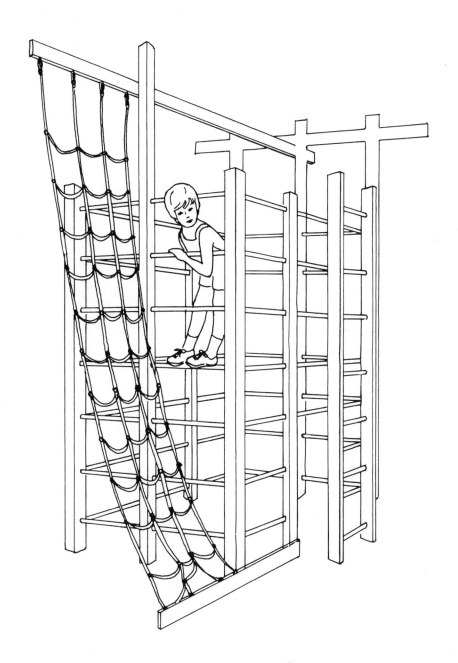

Platform with Cargo Net

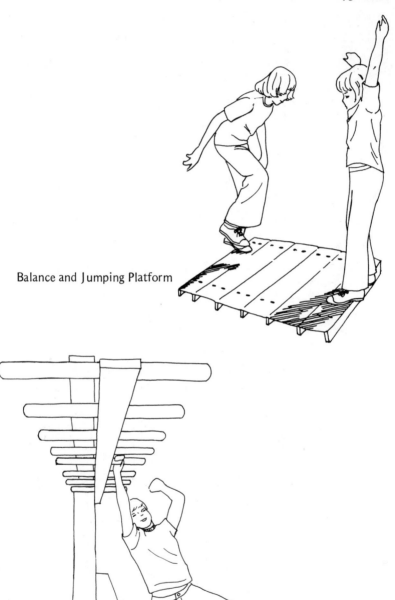

Balance and Jumping Platform

Platform with Climbing Rungs

Additional Ideas for Soft Surface Play Areas

Acquisition

Old boats, cars, trucks, fire engines, bathtubs, cement blocks, logs, and tree limbs can be used for children's creative play experiences. Don't be afraid to look around and get to know your community. Let people know you are a collector. People have to spot things and be recognized for the creative thought that leads to the recycling of throw-aways.

Construction

Prepare each piece of equipment for safe use on the playground. Take doors off of cars. Remove glass and sharp objects. On wood pieces remove splinters and worn parts. Anchor each piece securely to the ground. Use paint to decorate the equipment if you wish.

Ideas for use

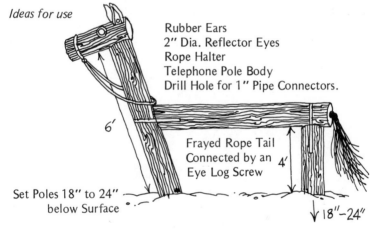

Rubber Ears
2" Dia. Reflector Eyes
Rope Halter
Telephone Pole Body
Drill Hole for 1" Pipe Connectors.

6'

Frayed Rope Tail
Connected by an
Eye Log Screw

4'

Set Poles 18" to 24"
below Surface

18"–24"

Materials   Telephone Pole 6"-8" in Diameter and 15' Long. Cut into 2'-4' sections, a 6' Section, and a 1' Section
1/2 " Dia. O.D. Pipe Connectors
3 Pieces, 16" Long
Ears — (2) Old Rubber Intertubes
Halter — Rope (Nylon or Hemp)
Eyes — (2) 2" Dia. Car Bumper Reflectors
Tail - (1) 3/8" x 4" Long Eye Lag Screw plus Old Frayed Rope

Many discarded items can be used for playground equipment.

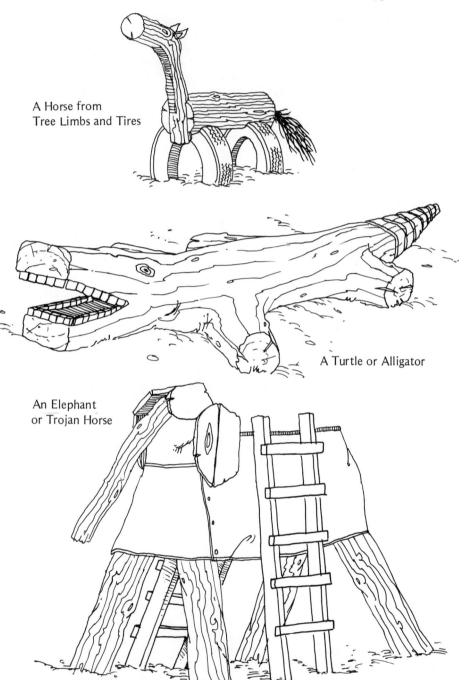

A Horse from
Tree Limbs and Tires

A Turtle or Alligator

An Elephant
or Trojan Horse

A Bathtub and Tire Car

An Old Jalopy

A Race Car Cut from Logs

An Old Rowboat

A Limb Sheltering a Sand Area

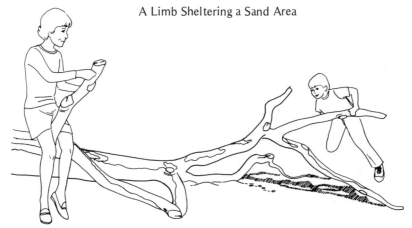

Limbs for Climbing

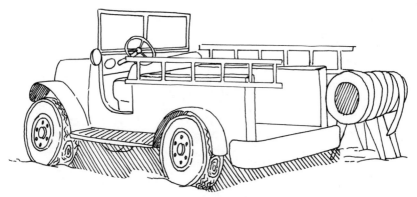

An Old Fire Engine

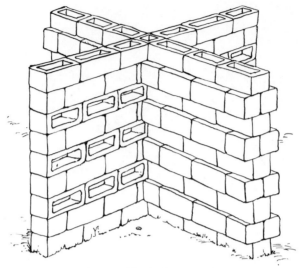

Cement Blocks for Climbing

Hard Surface Design Ideas

Acquisition

Purchase the paint you need from a local dealer. You may be able to get a discount if you tell him about your project.

Construction

Use a 2- to 4-inch brush to paint the desired designs on the pavement. White and yellow traffic paint works well. Other colors may also be used. Make an outline of the design on the surface with chalk before painting.

Ideas for designs

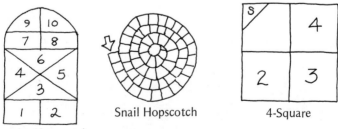

Regular Hopscotch   Snail Hopscotch   4-Square

Hard surface designs can be painted on the pavement.

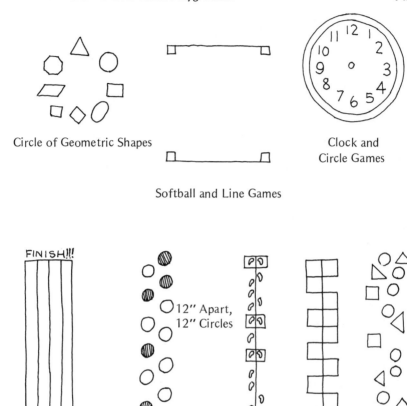

Circle of Geometric Shapes

Softball and Line Games

Clock and
Circle Games

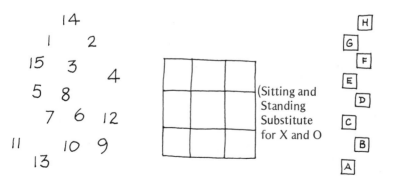

Running Lanes   Hop-the-Spots   Jumping and Hopping Mazes

12" Apart,
12" Circles

"Scattered" Numbers   "Human" Tic-Tac-Toe   Alphabet Stepping Stones

(Sitting and
Standing
Substitute
for X and O

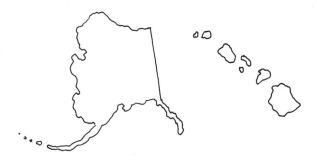

Map of United States: Jump, run or hop from state to state.

Bibliography

Aitken, Margaret H. *Play Environment for Children: Play, Space, Improvised Equipment and Facilities.* Bellingham, Wash.: Educational Designs and Consultants, 1972.

Christian, Quentin A. *The Beanbag Curriculum: A Homemade Approach to Physical Activity for Children.* Wolfe City, Tex.: The University Press, 1973.

Corbin, Charles B. *Inexpensive Equipment for Games, Play, and Physical Activity.* Dubuque, Iowa: W. C. Brown, 1972.

Dattner, Richard. *Design for Play.* New York: Van Nostrand Reinhold Company, 1969.

Dauer, Victor P., and Pangrazi, Robert P. *Dynamic Physical Education for Elementary School Children.* 5th ed. Minneapolis, Minn.: Burgess Publishing Company, 1975.

D'Eugenio, Terry. *Building with Tires.* Cambridge, Mass.: Advisory for Open Education, 1971.

Friedberg, M. Paul. *Playgrounds for City Children.* Washington, D.C.: Association for Childhood Education International, 1969.

Gallahue, David L. *Developmental Play Equipment for Home and School.* New York: John Wiley and Sons, Inc., 1975.

Gallahue, Davis L.; Werner, Peter H.; and Luedke, George C. *A Conceptual Approach to Moving and Learning.* New York: John Wiley and Sons, Inc., 1975.

Hogan, Paul. *Playgrounds for Free.* Cambridge, Mass.: The MIT Press, 1974.

Hurtwood, Lady Allen of. *Planning for Play.* Cambridge, Mass.: The MIT Press, 1968.

Kirchner, Glenn. *Physical Education for Elementary School Children.* Dubuque, Iowa: W. C. Brown, 1974.

Miller, Peggy L. *Creative Outdoor Play Areas.* Englewood Cliffs, N.J.: Prentice-Hall, Inc., 1972.

Pitts, Mabel B. *Tires Are Tools for Learning.* Austin, Tex.: State Department of Public Welfare, 1970.

Schurr, Evelyn L. *Movement Experiences for Children.* Englewood Cliffs, N.J.: Prentice-Hall, Inc., 1975.

Stone, Jeannette Galambos. *Play and Playgrounds.* Washington, D.C.: National Association for the Education of Young Children, 1970.

Vannier, Maryhelen; Foster, Mildred; and Gallahue, David L. *Teaching Physical Education in Elementary Schools.* Philadelphia: W. B. Saunders, 1973.

Werner, Peter H., and Rini, Liza. *Perceptual-Motor Development Equipment.* New York: John Wiley and Sons, Inc., 1976.

Appendix

Sources of Materials

Company	Materials
Adirondack Industries, Inc. Dolgeville, N.Y. 13329	Builder blocks, jumbo blocks, rocker walker, tunnel, large toys.
American Seating Grand Rapids, Mich. 49502	Building blocks, large manipulative toys, balance boards.
Childcraft Education Corp. P.O. Box 94 Bayonne, N.J. 07002	Builder blocks, climbing ropes and rope ladders, primary play dome, rhythm instruments.
Cosom Corporation 6030 Wayzata Boulevard Minneapolis, Minn. 55416	Plastic fun balls, rhythm and bounce balls, floor hockey sets, bowling sets, frisbees, plastic bats and hoops, aluminum stilts.
ED-NU, Inc. 5115 Route 38 Pennsauken, N.J. 08108	Plastic hoops.
Elliot-Morris Company 678 Washington Street Lynn, Mass. 01901	Plastic beanbags.

General Sportscraft Co. Ltd. 140 Woodbine Street Bergenfield, N.J. 07621	Variety of small equip- ment, paddles, beanbags, jump ropes, gym scooters, Indian clubs.
General Tire Box 951 Akron, Ohio 44309	Pennsylvania-brand game balls of all kinds includ- ing playground balls sizes 5 inches to 16 inches and junior footballs.
Interstate Rubber Products Corp. 908 Avila Street Los Angeles, Calif. 90012	Traffic cones.
Jayfro Corp. P.O. Box 400 Waterford, Conn. 06385	Peg boards.
New York Athletic Supply Company 301 East 149th Street Bronx, N.Y. 10451	Gym scooters.
Passon's Inc. 824 Arch Street Philadelphia, Pa. 19107	Gym scooters.
Playschool, Inc. Dept. E. Division of Milton Bradley Company 3720 North Kedzie Ave. Chicago, Ill. 60618	Preschool and primary durable toys, hardwood blocks, play cubes, block carts, and bins.
J. A. Preston 71 Fifth Avenue New York, N.Y. 10003	Parachute.
Program Aids 161 Mac Queen Parkwy. Mt. Vernon, N.Y. 10550	Parachute.

S.D.E., Co.   Vaulting boxes.
A subsidiary of Leisure
Enterprises, Inc.
1340 North Jefferson
Anaheim, Calif. 92806

A. G. Spalding and Bros.   Official game equip-
Inc.   ment, junior football.
Meadow Street
Chicopee, Mass. 01014

Star Division of V and S   Game standards, climbing
Industries Inc.   ropes, horizontal ladders
Box 480   and bars, small equipment.
Owosso, Mich. 48867

Sterling Recreation Products   Fun ball, playground balls,
7 Oak Place   plastic scoops, frisbees,
Montclair, N.J. 07042   beanbags, cargo nets.

Timberform   Wooden playground
1727 N.E. Eleventh Avenue   equipment.
Portland, Ore. 97212

R. E. Titus Gym Scooter Co.   Gym scooters.
Winfield, Kans. 67156

W. J. Voit Rubber Corp.   Small games equipment,
29 Essex Street   balls of many varieties
Maywood, N.J. 07607   including balls and junior
                                     footballs, jump ropes,
                                     batting tees.

Wilson Sporting Goods Co.   Official games equipment.
2233 West Street
River Grove, Ill. 60171

Wolters Co.   Polyethylene ball bags, skip
9250 South Buttonwillow   ropes, flag sets for tag games,
Reedley, Calif. 93654   indoor bases.

Worcester Braiding Company   Shock cord, elastic braid, nylon
Cherry Street   cord.
Hudson, Mass. 01749

Wolverine Sports Supply   Wide variety of small games
745 State Circle   equipment.
Ann Arbor, Mich. 48104

Climbing Equipment

Form Inc.   Sculptured forms for climbing,
12900 West Ten Mile Road   castle, turtle free forms.
South Lynn, Mich. 48178

Gaint Manufacturing Co.   Horizontal ladders, climbing
Council Bluffs, Iowa 51501   bars, balance beams, parallel
                              bars.

Game-Time Inc.   Geodesic climbing apparatus,
Litchfield, Mich. 49252   indoor obstacle course appara-
                              tus.

The Delmar F. Harris Co.   Jungle gym, climbing trees,
Concordia, Kans. 66901   uniladder ("Swedish gym").

Jamison Manufacturing Co.   Climbing ropes, monkey rings,
510 East Manchester Avenue   geodesic climbers, horizontal
Los Angeles, Calif. 90003   bars, tetherball standard,
                              backstops.

Miracle Equipment Company   Climbing apparatus, sculptured
Box 275   forms.
Grinnell, Iowa 50112

Northwest Design Products,   Cedar log and galvanized tube,
Inc.   indoor and outdoor play
1235 South Tacoma Way   structures.
Tacoma, Wash. 98409

Otto Industries PTY., Ltd.   Horizontal rope ladders, climb-
309-313 South Road   ing frames, climbing ropes,
Mile End South   portable gymnastic equipment.
Sth. Australia 5031

Playground Corporation of America 29-16 Fortieth Avenue Long Island City, N.Y. 11101	Sculptured and tubular play forms and play scapes, multi-purpose goal cages and backstops, game standards, sand boxes; playground designers.
Porter Equipment Co. 9555 Irving Park Road Schiller Park, Ill. 60176	Jungle gym climbers.
Recreation Equipment Corp. Anderson, Ind. 46011	Climbing equipment, horizontal ladders, and bars; also small equipment.

Index